Girish Karnad

A Contemporary Playwright

Shailaja B. Wadikar

ATLANTIC

PUBLISHERS & DISTRIBUTORS (P) LTD

Published by
ATLANTIC
PUBLISHERS & DISTRIBUTORS (P) LTD
7/22, Ansari Road, Darya Ganj, New Delhi-110002
Phones : +91-11-40775252, 23273880, 23275880, 23280451
Fax : +91-11-23285873
Web : www.atlanticbooks.com
E-mail : orders@atlanticbooks.com

Branch Office
5, Nallathambi Street, Wallajah Road, Chennai-600002
Phones : +91-44-64611085, 32413319
E-mail : chennai@atlanticbooks.com

Printed in India at Nice Printing Press, A-33/3A, Site-IV,
Industrial Area, Sahibabad, Ghaziabad, U.P.

To

Dr. Bhalchandra Nemade

and

Sow. Pratibha Nemade

Foreword

Modern drama is said to be a journey from realism to ritualism. It moves from the naturalism of Balzac, Flaubert and Zola to the realism of Ibsen, Strindberg, Chekhov and Shaw. Further, with the introduction of symbolism, under the influence of the French poet Mallarme, it takes altogether a new flight from realism to ritualism. Eliot, Yeats, Camus, Sartre, Beckett, etc. have given us the kind of drama we needed most—a new, avant-garde type of drama with existential overtones. It is not a great leap forward from these Anglo-French dramatists to the post-independence Indian dramatists such as Mohan Rakesh, Badal Sircar, Vijay Tendulkar and Girish Karnad

Girish Karnad is, of course, at the top, sharing a worldwide reputation with hardly any rivals in India. He is the one who can legitimately aspire for the award of the much-coveted Nobel Prize for literature. Like Zola, he too has pinned his faith in the dictum: "The theatre should not lie." He wants the theatre to serve the inquiring mind in investigating, analyzing and reporting on the man behind the facts, that is, the causal relationship of events—a systematic study of their causes and effects. Here, in Karnad's plays, we have coalescence of fact and fiction, reality and poetry, truth and beauty.

Girish Karnad is, perhaps, the greatest Kannada playwright of all India recognition. For the construction of his plot, he explores and exploits myth, history and folklore and brings out the play's relevance to the present times. In the structure of their plots and the treatment of their themes, the Karnad plays are, at once, simple and complex, like the Greek classical plays. The characterization is as individual as typical. As a result, the play's appeal is more intellectual than emotional. Both the classical and folk elements seem to happily merge with each other in the modernity of the plays under study.

Girish Karnad rarely confronts the reality face to face in his major plays. He prefers rather creating its illusion through myth, history and folklore. It is the world of imagination through which he approaches reality, however bare or stark it is. The relevance of his plays is, therefore, out of question—they are so obliquely, and so markedly, contemporaneous. From the formalist-cum-dramaturgical point of view, a Karnad play is of dual nature: readable and performable. So, it can be read in a closet and seen and heard in a theatre or on a TV screen.

Karnad's plays, under critical scrutiny here, are remarkable for their thematic treatment, plot-construction and characterization. There is deftness and subtlety in the depiction of situations and delineation of characters—both quite amazing. The plays' thematic structure operates more on the cognitive than on the emotional level. In consequence, it appeals more to the head than to the heart. "A fresh raid on the inarticulate" is how Eliot aptly describes the phenomenon. In the saint-poet Jnaneshwar's words, "that which is formless receives the form" at the hands of the dramatist. In the modernity of Karnad's plays, we have short, intermittent, passing glimpses of the classical and the folk theatres, simultaneously. For his themes and dramatic techniques, the playwright seems to rely solely on the use of history, myth and folklore.

Playwriting for Girish Karnad is a "maturing process", ripening not only physically but emotionally also, as if it were "a rite of passage". What pained him most is dehumanization of man by man. Thus, the playwright succeeds in establishing connectivity between the past and the present, by looking at the present as an extension of, and not an escape from, the past, by discovering the relevance of the past to the present events. Contemporaneity is the greatest source of Karnad's strength as a new playwright.

According to Brecht, the innovator of the term, "alienation effect", "the audience must be totally aware that it is in the theatre at all times." Despite the illusion of reality or verisimilitude it creates, he believes: "The motto of the new art…is, in one word, truth, and truth…is what we are striving for…." Thus, drama is, in its origin and nature, essentially didactic. It gives us a message, an inference, of course, at the level of the highest, that is, artistic communication.

In the vivid and realistic presentation of theme, plot, and characterization, Karnad stands apart from the rest of the dramatists in India. In all his plays, he is "as objective as a chemist", to quote Chekhov. It is with Chekhov, again, that he agrees and says: "I have not introduced a single villain nor an angel…I accused nobody, justified nobody." Thus, the new drama, as conceived by Girish Karnad, is characterized by truth and objectivity and stands for "plays, pleasant and unpleasant, to use the Shavian term".

While moving from realism to ritualism through symbolism, the Karnad theatre creates an illusion of reality, which is a great challenge in itself. The stage is, then, a great deal more than a mirror reflecting life in all its multifold aspects such as variety, ambiguity, maturity, complexity, tradition and modernity, etc. A symbol is a poetic device to clothe the thoughts with a sensory form. A ritual is steeped in symbols. That is why the theatre earns, through symbolism, a visionary quality that supersedes, rather transcends realism. There is as much showing here as telling. Thus, symbolism takes us beyond realism and towards surrealism, and, if you like, towards ritualism, in the ultimate analysis. That which is ineffable, incommunicable is communicated through symbols. Whether it is surrealism or ritualism—whatever name you give it—it dwells upon "inner reality" projected through the use of such dramatic devices as asides and soliloquies, pauses and silences, audio-visual effects and expressionistic techniques, leading to what Coleridge calls "willing suspension of disbelief" in his incisive art-criticism.

I have immense pleasure in congratulating Shailaja B. Wadikar upon her undertaking such a huge and comprehensive research project on the Girish Karnad theatre. I wish her great success in her academic enterprise!

L.S. Deshpande
Fellow, K.K. Birla
Foundation, New Delhi

Preface

Born on May 19, 1938, in Matheran, Maharashtra, Girish Karnad is India's leading playwright who has reshaped the Indian theatre as a major national institution in the last quarter of the twentieth century. He has won the national and international recognition as a playwright, poet, actor, translator, critic and ambassador of culture, the director of films and plays, television anchor and artist. He has eleven plays, two monologues, nine feature films, three documentaries, three tele-serials, one radio play and several articles and lectures to his credit. Beginning his career as a playwright in 1961, he is the winner of several national and international awards and honours including the Padma Bhushan, Sahitya Akademi, and India's highest literary award, the Bharatiya Jnanpith, etc.

The core content of the book is the analysis of the translated plays of Girish Karnad in terms of theme, plot, characterization, and world view. Majority of his plays are based on myth, history, and folklore. However, with their nativistic roots, the plays focus on tradition and modernity with a flood of light on the contemporary life and reality. The study aims at analyzing and examining the novel, revolutionary approach of Karnad with an eye on its validity and relevance.

In terms of form and content, the entire plays can be classified as: (i) the plays based on ancient myth (*Yayati*, *Bali: The Sacrifice*, and *The Fire and the Rain*), (ii) the plays based on the Indian history with contemporary relevance (*Tughlaq*, *Tale-Danda*, and *The Dreams of Tipu Sultan*), (iii) the plays based on folktales

(*Hayavadana*, *Nagamandala*, and *Flowers*), and (iv) the recent plays dealing with aspects of contemporary situations (*Broken Images*, *Wedding Album*, *Boiled Beans on Toast,* and *Driven Snow*). Among these, *Broken Images* and *Flowers* are monologues and the remaining ones are full-length plays.

The conflict between tradition and modernity forms the backbone of the Indian theatre. It mirrors a comparative critical scene of the pre-independence and the post-independence Indian drama, besides a brief note on the Karnataka theatre, Karnad's use of myth, history and folktales, followed by passing, comparative critical remarks on his fellow travellers—Mohan Rakesh, Badal Sircar and Vijay Tendulkar.

The play, *Yayati* deals with the theme of responsibility. It reinterprets an ancient Indian myth from the modernist, post-modernist point of view. The play focuses on man's "existential angst" along with his struggle for existence. It is an autobiographical play as it reflects the playwright's anxieties, his resentment with all those who seemed to demand, in sheer love of him, the sacrifice of his future.

The play, *Bali*: *The Sacrifice* discusses multiplicity of themes such as man-woman relationship, woman's position in male-dominated society, violence and non-violence, love and sex, tradition versus modernity, hatred, treachery, superstition, etc. The play deals with a debate on violence and non-violence which is deftly interlinked with man-woman relationship and thereby exposes meaninglessness and hollowness of courtly life. The central concern in the play is the message that intended violence is as much offensive as actual violence.

The Fire and the Rain depicts the negative impulses of a human being such as anger, violence, bloodshed, jealousy, pride, false knowledge, the intense feeling of hostility, hatred, greed, treachery and revenge. Here, Karnad finds the myth quite relevant to the contemporary society. The play communicates the message that abuse of knowledge ultimately leads to the destruction of the world. It vividly portrays the conflict between the orthodox Brahmin community and the benevolent tribal community.

The play, *Tughlaq* discusses in detail the mood of political disillusionment the country faced after the Nehru era of idealism. Historically, it was the story of the most intelligent and visionary Sultan of Delhi, who, in his attempts to fulfil his ideals, perpetuated hatred and violence.

Tale-Danda highlights the most delicate and crucial problem of caste system that has remained burning through all the ages of the Indian history. All the efforts of Basavanna of creating an egalitarian society come to nothing when he performs the marriage of a Dalit boy with a Brahmin girl. Actually, the socio-political events have prompted Karnad to write this play. It is not difficult to find the echoes of the contemporary political events in the royalist regime of Kalyan.

The Dreams of Tipu Sultan shows the Sultan's efforts towards nationalism. It represents the legendary hero Tipu Sultan, who dreams of his motherland and its independence which cannot be transformed into reality.

Hayavadana represents man's tragically futile aspiration for perfection through the dramatic version of a folktale. It is a Brechtian kind of play employing native folk theatre strategies to present the mysterious aspects of love and sex with a lot of doubtfulness and suspense.

Nagamandala criticizes gender-biased values and morals of the patriarchal society, where women have been oppressed for centuries together. Appanna and Naganna are actually the two aspects of man's nature—the one, seen during the day who performs the role of a dictator—and the other, at night, who plays the lover's role. These two contradictory faces symbolize the exploitation and double standards of man. Rani is the evidence of a woman's endless suffering in the male-dominated society.

Flowers is the work by Karnad having a male protagonist with two women playing minor roles. It is originally written in

English and then translated into Kannada by Karnad himself as "Hoovu". The monologue delves deep into the unfathomable depths of human mind and reflects its basic craving for love and sex which man tries to restrain for some social as well as individual obligations. Listening to his soul, the priest remarks, "God must understand, I simply cannot live on His terms" (260) and, ultimately, sacrifices his life by committing suicide.

In *Broken Images*, Karnad explores the contemporary reality to discuss such issues as plagiarism, politics of language, supremacy of literary genre, and the question of identity. Actually, the simulated image on the screen symbolically represents the protagonist's inner voice, her conscience, her alter-ego that gives her a feel of guilt and crushes her pride ruthlessly.

Away from myths, folktales, and history, in *Wedding Album*, Karnad deals with contemporary Indian society with a view to exhuming the reality of Indian culture and the politics of the tele-serials and internet cafés, used as a means for the fulfilment of erotic fantasies. Reading or observing the play seems like turning the photographs in an album of the Indian culture.

Boiled Beans on Toast, the latest play by Karnad, revolves round the unsung tales of ordinary Bengaluru citizens and their struggles. No doubt, the play's title is linked with a myth but the play marks a total departure from Karnad's famous plays steeped in historical and mythological themes. The chief protagonist of the play is the city of Bengaluru, adversely affected by globalization: "This is the city of wild hopes and dashed dreams, of disappointment and despair, of environmental destruction and rapid development."

Driven Snow is the only play with a non-Indian locale. It projects the plight of those who choose to cross the borders of motherland and venture to settle down in a foreign land. Likewise, it speaks of all those who also choose to cross the borders, by breaking the taboos, within India. Karnad, here, ventures upon a courageous action of exploring the incestuous relationship that exists between a sister and her brother. Every time, the signs get erased, giving place to the new ones to establish the phenomenal work.

The dramatic movement in the post-independence period, particularly of the post-1960 generation, has transformed itself, shifting from its regional character to the pan-Indian one. Karnad has succeeded in setting new trends in Indian drama. He seems to be very close to T.S. Eliot, who, by advocating adherence to history and tradition, holds allegiance to humanity. He maintains the preservation of the good in tradition while breaking away from it. Majority of his plays throw light on his strong historical sense, which impels him to speak of "the pastness of the past" for it is outdated, and to welcome the presence of the past that is visible in the living present. Some of his plays are classic in the sense that they dissolve the boundaries between the temporality and eternity. They are par excellence and have set a high watermark of dramatics and dramaturgy.

The climax of Karnad's dramatic career will be the day when he wins the much-coveted Noble Prize for literature in the near future. It will not be an exaggeration to say that his versatile genius makes one feel that, long after Gurudev Tagore, it is he who deserves it more than anyone else.

Shailaja B. Wadikar

Acknowledgements

I wish to put on record my special thanks to Girish Karnad for his kindly gesture of giving me the manuscript of his unpublished play, *Driven Snow* and for providing me with the information about his latest published play. His words in the mail are a great source of perennial joy and inspiration for me.

My sincere thanks go to all those who helped me directly or indirectly in the completion of this book. I take this opportunity to express a sense of gratitude to all the writers whose works I dwelt upon while writing this book and the two institutions that cooperated me a lot in the completion of the book: S.R.T.M. University, Nanded and Indian Institute of Advanced Studies, Shimla. My heartfelt thanks are also due to my family, my revered Guru Dr. L.S. Deshpande, and friends. Last but not least, I am thankful to the Atlantic Publishers & Distributors (P) Ltd., New Delhi for the interest evinced in publishing this book.

Shailaja B. Wadikar
29, Bhagyanagar, Nanded-431 605
Cell: 09890275257, 08055878315
shailaja_wadikar@yahoo.co.in
shailajawadikar7@gmail.com

Contents

NEW PLAYS

EPILOGUE

PROLOGUE

1

Tradition and Modernity

Indian Drama: A Brief Survey

India is an ancient country known for her variety of cultures, customs, languages and literatures. It has a gigantic and rich dramatic tradition of its own. However, it is difficult to trace the origin of the Indian drama and determine the specific date or year of its inception. The journey of Indian drama starts with the Classical Sanskrit plays. Therefore, its origin can be traced back to the ancient times. About two thousand years ago, we had our own theory of drama known as *Natyashastra* by Bharatamuni. The two great epics of India, the *Ramayana* and the *Mahabharata* have inspired many creative writers for centuries together. At the very beginning, the Indian drama relied for its sources on the epic and mythical literature and was, therefore, closely linked to the Hindu religious and philosophical tradition.

The Classical Sanskrit drama gave us a few renowned playwrights like Asvaghosa, Bhasa, Kalidasa, Bhavabhuti, Sudraka, Visakhadatta and Harsha. The period in which these playwrights produced their plays was regarded as the rich and the golden age of Sanskrit drama.

The earliest Sanskrit plays were based on the Vedas and Upanishads. In our ancient classical literature, drama has been regarded as 'the fifth Veda' and it is pertinently termed as the 'Drishya Kaavya' (visual poetry). Taking recitation from the Rig Veda, imitation from Yajur Veda, melody from Sama Veda there was born the fifth Veda called Nataka or Drishya Kaavya. To it, Siva contributed "tandava" dance of violent emotion, Parvati contributed "Lasya" of tender feeling, and Vishnu contributed the four dramatic styles. Indra and the other gods requested

Brahma to provide entertainment that could restore the health of the society. (In Appendix 1 to the *Collected Plays,* Vol. 2, in his note on *The Fire and the Rain*, Karnad also gives the details of the birth of drama.)

The Sanskrit plays like *Abhijnana-Sakuntalam, Vikramorvasiyam* of Kalidasa; *Swapanavasavadattam* of Bhasa; *Uttararamacharita* of Bhavabhuti and *Venisamhara* and *Mudrarakshasa* of Visakhadatta are some of the worth-noting plays. In fact, they form an imperishable part of our literary heritage. However, from the seventh century onwards, there was noticeable decline in the quality and originality in playwriting in Sanskrit. With the decline of the Sanskrit drama, in the medieval times, the folk theatre in regional languages started dominating the stage.

Later on it was Sri Sankara, a saint-philosopher tried to revive and revitalize the Vedic religion and culture. He preached the importance of religion which obviously gave rise to the Bhakti cult. Indians were known for their cultural heritage and religious fervour; they held the religion and Vedas in high esteem. Thereafter, the Indian saints like Tukaram, Ramadas, Kabir, Chaitanya, Tulsidas, and Basaveshwara also highlighted the importance of Bhakti. The spread of Bhakti as a pan-Indian cult was chiefly responsible for various kinds of popular dramatic performances in various regions of the country, namely *Ramlila, Raslila* and *Nautanki* of North, *Tamasha* of Maharashtra, *Bhavai* of Gujarat, *Jatra* of Bengal and *Yakshagana* of Karnataka, etc. Apart from the stories from the epics and legends of the country, satires on men, manners and morals also formed the theme of these performances. In this way, in the process of evolution of the Indian drama, the Classical Sanskrit drama and the folk theatre made a great impact upon each other. These dramatic performances were followed by translations of Sanskrit plays into regional languages. With the establishment of the British regime in India, a search for a new theatre was strongly felt.

Further, the British education made its everlasting impact on the social structure of the country. The most vital thing is that the war of Independence of 1857 gave rise to a new awakening among the people. As a result, a number of twentieth-century writers gave a new turn to the Indian writing and thought expressing the contemporary urge for freedom. In this way, drama served as an instrument for bringing about awareness among the common people of the country.

Indian English plays and playwrights can be divided broadly into two phases—the pre-independence and the post-independence.

(A) THE PRE-INDEPENDENCE INDIAN ENGLISH DRAMA

In the Indian English Literature, drama failed to register an appreciable growth. English, being a foreign language, was difficult to understand and to use as a medium of creative writing. So, the playwrights found it difficult to write natural and graceful dialogues in colloquial English. Still, some Indian English playwrights made a sincere, earnest effort to write plays in English.

The pre-independence era witnessed eminent playwrights like Rabindranath Tagore, Sri Aurobindo, T.P. Kailasam, Harindranath Chattopadhyaya and Bharati Sarabhai who made substantial contribution to the growth of the Indian English drama. The playwrights of this period discussed the problems of the contemporary society with the use of history, legend, epic, and myth.

Rabindranath Tagore and Sri Aurobindo, the two renowned poets of India, were the first Indian dramatists in English worth considering. It is important to note the fact that Rabindranath Tagore, Sri Aurobindo, and Harindranath Chattopadhyaya are known as the 'big three' in the realm of Indian English drama.

The Indian English drama can be studied in its two-fold forms: (i) the plays originally written in English and (ii) the plays translated into English.

(i) The Plays Originally Written in English

The first Indian English play was *The Persecuted* (1831) by Krishna Mohan Banerjee. It depicted the theme of the East-West encounter and juxtaposed the conflict between Indian orthodox thought and the new Western idea. Michael Madhusudan Dutt's

Is This Called a Civilization? dealt with the contemporary problems of day-to-day life.

Sri Aurobindo, a significant contemporary of Tagore, wrote plays directly in English and played sedulous ape to the blank verse drama of the Elizabethans. He, too, was a versatile genius not only proficient in the great classics of Greece, Rome, France, and Spain but also fully acquainted with the rich Sanskrit Literature. He was a great creative artist with abundant knowledge of Indian philosophy, culture, and society. *Perseus, The Deliverer* (1942), *Vasavadutta* (1957), *Rodogune* (1958), *The Viziers of Bassora* (1959) and *Eric* (1960) are complete plays which underscore the need for love as love alone is the great remedy for all forms of evil.

Sri Aurobindo was highly influenced by the Shakespearian tragedy, the Jacobean tragedy, and the Bible. However, his longest play *Perseus, the Deliverer* was inspired by his participation in the freedom struggle of India. Here, he depicted the agonies and sufferings of freedom fighters. Aurobindo's plays had a variety of themes and well-designed structure but most of them remained closet dramas.

The last name of the 'Big Three' in the realm of Indian English drama is Harindranath Chattopadhyaya. He is one of the multifaceted playwrights of the contemporary Indian society. His dramatic output could be classified as devotional plays, social plays, historical plays and miscellaneous plays. His seven plays entitled as *Poems and Plays* (1927) dealing with the lives of some Maharashtrian saints, could be incorporated in the category of devotional plays. They are: *Raidas, Chokhamela, Eknath, Pundalik, Sakubai, Jayadeva,* and *Tukaram.* They are all written in verse, and are playlets rather than full-length plays. The first play, *Raidas* deals with the cobbler-saint of that name. And *Tukaram*, the last one in this group is said to be the best in terms of characterization and plot construction. The most significant of Harindranath's social plays are found in his collection of *Five Plays* (1937). They are: *The Window, The Parrot, The Sentry's Lantern, The Coffin,* and *The Evening Lamp. The Window* and *The Parrot* depict the playwright's acute awareness of the social problems. In *The Sentry's Lantern*, the dramatist symbolically expresses the hope of the dawn of a new era for the poor. *The Coffin* satirizes the world of the bourgeois artist, and *The Evening Lamp* reflects the contemporary social situation.

The major themes of Harindranath Chattopadhyaya's plays are sympathy for the exploited, revolt against the useless codes of morality, and the evil forces of imperialism. He wrote some devotional and historical plays; majority of his plays were of social nature, reflecting the contemporary social situation. It was for this reason that Iyengar called his plays: "manifestoes of the new dawn of realism".[1]

A.S.P. Ayyar was also a notable playwright who wrote six plays on social and reformist themes. Some of his famous plays are: *In the Clutch of the Devil* (1926), *Trial of Science for the Murder of Humanity* (1943), *Sita's Choice and Other Plays* (1935), *The Slaves of Ideas and Other Plays* (1941). *Sita's Choice and Other Plays* deals with a social problem of the remarriage of a widow. In Ayyar's plays, the purpose is more important than craftsmanship.

T.P. Kailasam is also a prominent playwright in the Indian English Literature. The epics, the *Ramayana* and the *Mahabharata*, provided plots for his English plays. He had an excellent knowledge of the English and Western dramatic traditions. He wrote both in Kannada and English. His English plays are: *The Burden* (1933), *Fulfilment* (1933), *The Purpose* (1944), *Karna or The Brahmin's Curse* (1946), *Keechaka* (1949) and *A Monologue: Don't Cry* (1933). In his English plays, he employs classical themes that deal with contemporary issues. His subtle power of observation and deep understanding of human nature enable him to create convincing characters like Polee Kitti, Ranganna, Nagatte, and Satu. As a playwright, he reveals an excellent fusion of genius and intuitive vision. He had a great power of imagination and a thorough knowledge of theatre.

So far as the pre-independence era is concerned, among the few women playwrights, only name that seems to be worth considering is that of Bharati Sarabhai. She was profoundly influenced by the Gandhian philosophy. So, her first verse play *The Well of the People* (1943) clearly reflects the impact of Gandhi. It deals basically with the theme of untouchability. The protagonist is portrayed vaguely and her thoughts and actions lack vigour and vitality. Her second play *Two Women* (1952), written in prose, realistically presents a picture of Indian womanhood. There is a fine blending of the material and the spiritual world in the play.

J.M. Lobo Prabhu seems to be the significant name in pre-independence Indian English drama. He wrote a number of plays but only two plays, *Mother of New India: A Play of the Indian Village in Three Acts* (1944) and *Death Abdicates* (1945) appeared before Independence. His *Collected Plays* was published in 1956. He is well-known for his skilful dialogue writing and creating admirable situations. However, his characters do not appear life-like and convincing.

Apart from the major playwrights of the pre-independence era, a few more names of playwrights may be taken into consideration, though they have made a little contribution to the Indian English drama. Among them are: S. Fyzee-Rahamin (*Daughter of the Ind*), Sudhindra N. Ghose (*Colours of a Great City* and two playlets—*The Defaulters* and *Pippa Dances*), R.K. Narayan (*The Watchman of the Lake*), K.R.S. Iyengar (*The Storm in a Tea-cup* and *The Battle of the Optionals*), D.K. Roy (*Life of Chaitanya*), Balwant Gargi (*The Vultures and the Other Plays*), and Mrinalini Sarabhai (*The Captive Soil*).

(ii) The Plays Translated into English

Rabindranath Tagore is a prolific dramatist who himself translated most of his Bengali plays into English. All these appeared in *Collected Poems and Plays* (1936). His plays are mainly known for their originality and for skilful blending of spiritualism, symbolism, and lyrical quality. His plays are categorized as: (a) symbolic, (b) devotional, and (c) problem plays. Tagore seems to be greatly impressed by Shakespeare and Ibsen and tries to follow their modes and techniques in his plays.

Tagore's widely-acclaimed plays *The Post Office* (1914) and *The King of the Dark Chamber* (1914) in Bengali were translated, respectively, by Devabrata Mukhopadhyaya and K.C. Sen into English. Some of the earliest plays of Tagore are *Sanyasi* (*The Ascetic*, 1884), *The King and the Queen* (1889), *Sacrifice* (1890), *Chitra* (1892), *Karna and Kunti* (1897) and *Gandhari's Prayer* (1897).

The plays *Ascetic* and *Sacrifice* exposed the social evils. In *Sacrifice*, he condemned the sacrifice of people by accepting outdated customs and traditions. His later plays such as *The King of the Dark Chamber* (1914), *The Waterfall* (*Mukta-Dhara*, 1922), *The Red Oleanders* (1925) and *The Post Office* (1914) were written in the allegorical and symbolic mode, and were considered to be his most vital contribution as a dramatist. He also wrote a number of romantic playlets based on the Buddhist themes. They are *Malini* (1912), *The Worship of the Dancing Girl* (*Natir Puja*, 1926), and *The Untouchable Girl* (*Chandalika*, 1933).

Besides being a great poet and playwright, he was an actor and a theatre artist well-versed in the great dramatic tradition. Greatly influenced by Kalidasa, Shakespeare, and Ibsen, he tried to bring coordination between the East and the West.

The growth and development of the Indian drama originally written in English remained poor and lopsided. Though the translated plays of Tagore, Madhusudan Dutt contributed a lot to the development of the Indian English drama, the "problems of language and translation have affected some of Tagore's plays. Moreover, his English translations lack the flavour and spirit of the originals in Bengali."[2]

Michael Madhusudan Dutt, a Bengali writer, translated plays such as *Ratnawali, Sermista,* etc. His devotional plays were based on the lives of the Indian saints. Despite the remarkable and abiding contribution of Tagore, Aurobindo and Chattopadhyaya, Indian English drama has never reached the high status of prose fiction or poetry. The dramatists have not solved the problem of fusing dramatic stories with dialogues and a sense of good theatre, all of which are indispensable to the success of a play on the stage.

For the growth of English drama, several European touring companies visited India and performed plays in Mumbai. The upshot of it was that many amateur groups and clubs flourished in the decade between 1860 and 1870. However, most of the plays were comedies, farces, operas that were not in harmony with the contemporary mood of the people. So, all these efforts, individually and cumulatively, could not contribute to the growth of English drama in India. Instead, their activities contributed a lot to the growth of the Marathi and Gujarati drama. English drama failed to meet the challenge of the regional language drama. The ultimate result of it was the decline of the original English drama in India in the pre-independence period.

(B) THE POST-INDEPENDENCE INDIAN ENGLISH DRAMA

The post-independence Indian English drama also can be studied in its two-fold forms like that of the pre-independence one: (i) The plays originally written in English and (ii) The plays translated into English.

(i) The Plays Originally Written in English

During the early phase of the post-independence period also, there has been no notable development in Indian English drama. However, one important thing about the plays written in this period is that they show a greater impact of the West. It appears that the playwrights of this period have made various types of experiments in handling the themes and characters and also in employing new models and techniques. Initially, they did not get a chance for staging their plays. Most of the theatres were occupied by the plays written in regional languages. Indian English plays were given only occasional performances. There was, in fact, no regular school of Indian English drama. However, during this period, the westerners showed their keen interest in Indian literature in general and Indian English drama in particular. Some of the plays written by the prominent playwrights like Asif Currimbhoy, Pratap Sharma, and Gurucharan Das received a good response in the West. A few plays like Das' *Mira*, Pratap Sharma's *A Touch of Brightness* and Asif Currimbhoy's *The Dumb Dancer* were successfully staged in Europe and U.S.A. It was really a remarkable achievement. In India, the Theatre

Group in Mumbai and other agencies also staged the plays of these playwrights. It is to be noted that in the post-independence period, most of the plays were written in prose. However, some playwrights like G.V. Desani, P.A. Krishnaswamy, Manjeri Isvaran, Lakhan Deb and Pritish Nandy were drawn to poetic drama. G.V. Desani's *Hali* (1950) is the finest poetic play of this period which received great appreciation for its rich imagery and symbolism. It is an autobiographical play which depicts a serious love affair. It was successfully staged in London and India. P.A. Krishnaswamy's *The Flute of Krishna* (1950) is another poetic play which depicts a devotee's unflinching faith in God. Manjeri Isvaran's *Yama and Yami* (1948) written in poetic prose brings out the incestuous love of Yami for her brother. Lakhan Deb has written three verse plays: *Tiger Claw* (1967), *Vivekanand* (1972) and *Murder at the Prayer Meeting* (1976). *Tiger Claw* and *Murder at the Prayer Meeting* are historical plays. The first one is about the killing of Afzal Khan by Shivaji and the second one, showing great impact of T.S. Eliot, is concerned with the assassination of Mahatma Gandhi. It is noticed that the number of prose playwrights is larger than that of the verse playwrights.

Asif Currimbhoy is one of the notable playwrights in Indian writing in English. He has published about thirty plays, the first of them being *The Tourist Mecca* (1959). He is a prolific writer focusing the various subjects like contemporary politics, social and economic problems, the East-West encounter, psychological tension, Indian philosophy, religion, and art. Currimbhoy's social concerns are clearly reflected in his plays, *The Doldrummers* (1962), *Thorns on a Canvas* (1968), *The Hungry Ones* (1965) and *The Miracle Seed* (1973). *The Doldrummers*, a play in two acts, was banned by the government soon after its publication but later on the ban was lifted. It was presented on the stage in 1969 by the Little Theatre Group in Delhi. The major political events which attracted Currimbhoy's attention are the partition and its aftermath in *The Captives* (1968), the liberation of Goa from the Portuguese domination in *Goa: A Tragedy in Two Acts* (1964), Indian freedom movement in *An Experiment with Truth* (1969), the Naxalite movement in *Inquilab* (1970), the Bangladesh war in *The Refugee* (1971), the student unrest in Gujarat in *The Dissident M.L.A.* (1974), and the birth of Bangladesh in *Sonar Bangala* (1972). In short, Currimbhoy incorporates all the contemporary issues in the post-independence period in his plays. Therefore, he is one of the most remarkable playwrights in the contemporary Indian English drama.

The contribution of Mahasweta Devi, renowned Bengali playwright, should also be taken into consideration. She has written several plays of which *Mother of 1084* (a novel, later on converted into drama), *Urvashi O Johnny*, *Aajir*, *Bayen* and *Water* are worth noticing. Mahasweta seeks to throw light on the predicament of the individuals placed in different social situations. Her plays show her commitment and concern for the downtrodden sections of the society who are deprived of their basic rights. She fights for the Dalits and tribals. Her non-dramatic especially activist writings, also reveal her concern for human rights and dignity of man.

The other notable playwrights writing originally in English in the post-independence era are Pratap Sharma, Nissim Ezekiel, Gurucharan Das, Gieve Patel, Lakhan Deb, M.V. Rama Sarma, Santha Rama Rau, Manjula Padmanabhan, and Dina Mehta. Pratap Sharma's plays *A Touch of Brightness* (1968) and *The Professor has a War Cry* (1970) criticize social hypocrisy. The most outstanding of them is Mahesh Dattani. His plays become successful on the stage in the foreign land. Sex seems to be the major theme of his plays.

Nissim Ezekiel's three plays *Nalini: A Comedy*, *Marriage Poem: A Tragedy*, *The Sleep Walkers: An Indo-American Farce* (1969) are remarkable for bold thematic experiments and masterly use of irony and fantasy. *Son of Deprivation*, a short play was also published in 1969. The main feature of Ezekiel's plays is a skilful use of the ironic, fantastic use of dramatic strategies and techniques.

Gurucharan Das' *Larins Sahib* (1970) is a historical play which deals with nineteenth-century colonial India. *Mira* (1971) portrays the saint Mira's selfless love for Lord Krishna which was successfully produced as a ballet in New York, and as a play in Bombay. His play, *Jakhoo Villa* deals with the theme of decadence in modern Hindu family in Shimla.

There are other important Indian English playwrights in this phase who have contributed in their own ways to the growth and development of Indian English drama. M.V. Rama Sarma's *Collected Plays* (1982) is a group of eleven plays on divergent subjects. *Youth and Crabbed Age*, *Like to Like*, and *This Busy World* are his playlets in which the impact of Bernard Shaw is strongly felt. *Shakuntala, Marpessa,* and *Urvasi* are plays dealing with the theme of love. *Towards Marriage* (1954) and *The Carnival* are both realistic and satirical. *The Mahatma* (1979) deals with the martyrdom of Mahatma Gandhi.

Santha Rama Rau's play *A Passage to India* is modelled upon E.M. Forster's famous novel *A Passage to India.* M. Krishnamurti's *The Cloth of Gold* (1951) is a dance drama set in feudal times. K.S.R. Sastri's *Droupadi* is a very interesting retelling of the Mahabharata story. D.M. Borgaonkar's *Image Breakers* (1938) is a problem play on the marriage institution. The other plays worth considering are Manohar Malgonkar's *Line of Mars* (1971), V.K. Gokak's *The Goddess Speaks* (1948), Nagarajan's *Chidambaram: A Chronicle Play* (1955), Shiv K. Kumar's *The Last Wedding Anniversary* (1975), V.D. Trivedi's *My Forest* (1963), Ahmed Akhtar's *Anarkali* (1978), Dina Mehta's *The Myth-makers* (1969), Arati Nagarwalla's *The Bait* (1969), Kamala Das' *A Mini-Trilogy* (1971), K.S. Rangappa's *Gandhiji's Sadhana* (1969), Murlidas Melwani's *Deep Roots* (1970), Dilip Hero's *To Anchor a Cloud* (1972), P.S. Vasudev's *Lord Ravan of Lanka* (1974), Syed Amanuddin's *The King Who Sold his Wife* (1978), K.S. Duggal's *To Each a Window: Six Radio Plays* (1981), and Masti Venkatesa Iyengar's *Kalidasa* (1980), etc. The efforts made by these playwrights reveal the fact that the future of Indian English drama is certainly bright and optimistic.

Mahesh Dattani, a contemporary Indian playwright writing originally in English, deals with such bold themes as sexuality and homosexuality. He boldly handles the tabooed subjects in his plays and produces them on stage for public discussion. In

1998, he won the Sahitya Akademi Award for his play *Final Solutions and Other Plays*. He is well-known for his contribution as a playwright, an actor, a director, a dancer, and a teacher. The first volume includes plays such as *Seven Steps around the Fire*, *On a Muggy Night in Mumbai*, *Final Solutions*, *Tara*, *Dance Like a Man,* etc. and the second volume including two earlier plays contains plays such as *Thirty Days in September*, *Clearing the Rubble*, *Mango Souffle*, *The Swami and Winston*, *Morning Raga*, *Uma and the Fairy Queen*, *Ek Alag Mausam* and *The Tale of a Mother Feeding her Child*. His plays bring forth some of the important problems of the modern society like sex, religion, communal violence, feminine identity, homosexuality and lesbian relationship, crime, horrible diseases like AIDS, etc. Therefore, his plays appear to be revolting and sometimes outrageous, too. Apart from the burning, contemporary issues, he shows his love of music and dance. The love of music and passion for dance are depicted through the protagonists of *Dance Like a Man* and *Morning Raga*. Dattani, being himself a stage performer, lays stress on theatricalities and the performance of the actor. He focuses on the mean, ugly, unpleasant, abominable aspects of human life.

Manjula Padmanabhan's pioneering play *Harvest* won Onassis Award and achieved world-wide popularity. It seriously portrays the mean and inhuman world in the metropolitan city like Mumbai where mothers sell their children in exchange for the handful of rice. She has also written five monologues entitled *Hidden Fires* which brings out violence in its various forms prevalent in the society. Both, Dattani and Padmanabhan, are dynamic and promising theatre personalities. They have certainly contributed to the growth and development of Indian English drama.

(ii) The Plays Translated into English

In the latter half of the 19th century, several plays in regional languages were translated into English and established a cultural link between the East and the West. The Indian playwrights Girish Karnad in Kannada, Mohan Rakesh in Hindi, Badal Sircar in Bengali, and Vijay Tendulkar, Satish Alekar, G.P. Deshpande,

Mahesh Elkunchwar, and Datta Bhagat, etc. in Marathi noticed that Indian literature was an entity in itself despite the fact that it was written in many languages. One of the reasons of the popularity of their plays was their sincere, truthful projection of contemporary life.

These dramatists made bold innovations and fruitful experiments and stimulated the growth of the Indian national theatre movement. They have used themes related to the present social scenario in order to bring about social change and make people aware of the need to renovate or reconstruct the present social structure. Broadly speaking, a number of twentieth century writers have given a new turn to Indian writing and thought. Contemporary Indian writing is rich, complex, and stimulating.

The playwrights of the Experimental Theatre mark a definite break with the playwrights of the previous generation. Vigorous attempts have been made to bring realism in theme, structure, setting, and dialogues. So, contemporary daily life remains the source of inspiration. Films also have a profound influence on the form and structure of the play. The original and translated works of such playwrights and directors as Utpal Dutt, Badal Sircar, Girish Karnad, C.T. Khanolkar, Sadanand Rege, Amol Palekar, Vijay Tendulkar, Satish Alekar, Mahesh Elkunchwar, Vijaya Mehta, Sai Paranjape, etc. have contributed a lot to the development of the Experimental Theatre in India.

The playwrights such as Tendulkar, Elkunchwar, and Alekar, in their plays, follow the dramatic techniques of Brecht, Beckett, and Ionesco and, as such, they represent the theatre of the avant-garde, the absurd in Marathi, of course, within their own limits.

Satish Alekar's best-known play *Mahanirwan*, translated into English by Gauri Deshpande, is a black comedy. Using the incident of a funeral, he satirizes the outdated customs, traditions, and religious orthodoxy. His other plays translated into English are *Mahapur, Atireki, Begum Barve*, etc. All these plays differ in subject-matter but each of them treats the absurd in a big or small way.

Mahesh Elkunchwar's *Wasanakand, Garbo, Wada Chirebandi, Party*, and *Atmakatha* are noteworthy translated plays. *Garbo* is an absurd play; *Wasanakand* is a static play with a scant and slow-moving action, based on Freudian psycho analysis.

G.P. Deshpande's *Udhwasta Dharmashala* and C.T. Khanolkar's *Ek Shoonya Bajirao* are also the remarkable translated plays. *Ek Shoonya Bajirao* (*Bajirao, the Cipher*), though an absurd play, has been a great success in the Experimental Theatre in the Indian context.

Datta Bhagat, one of the pioneers of Dalit theatre, gets an international recognition for his play *Routes and Escape Routes* (*Wata, Palwata* in Marathi). His plays deal with the universal inhuman suffering of the downtrodden outcaste within the caste-bound hierarchy of Indian society.

The post-independence playwrights seem to be greatly influenced by the dramatic style of Euro-American playwrights such as Henric Ibsen, Bernard Shaw, Anton Chekhov, T.S. Eliot, Albert Camus, Bertolt Brecht, Jean-Paul Sartre, Tennessee Williams, Arthur Miller, Edward Albee, etc. These Indian playwrights, who truly present the modern Indian sensibility, have been acclaimed as the pioneers of modern Indian drama. The major focus here is on the feelings and experiences of the ordinary men engaged in their day-to-day struggle for existence.

Among the regional playwrights, Girish Karnad is one who himself has translated his plays into brilliant, fluid English. His contribution to the Indian theatre can be traced in the structure of his plays such as *Yayati*, *Bali: The Sacrifice, The Fire and the Rain, Tughlaq, Tale-Danda, The Dreams of Tipu Sultan, Hayavadana, Nagamandala, Flowers, Broken Images, Wedding Album, Boiled Beans on Toast* and *Driven Snow*. Vijay Tendulkar, a noted screen and television playwright is considered to be a vanguard[3] of the Indian theatre. Badal Sircar is an eminent Bengali playwright who has written more than forty-five plays some of which have been translated into English such as *Evam Indrajit, Bhoma, Stale News, There's No End, Procession, That Other History, Indian History Made Easy,* etc. Mohan Rakesh, writing originally in Hindi, has made a notable contribution to the Indian theatre with his plays such as *One Day in Ashadha, The Great Swans of the Waves,* and *Half Way House*.

Thus, the decade 1960-70 assumed significance in the history of the Indian English theatre, since plays written in Hindi, Bengali, Kannada, and Marathi were being translated into English and other languages. The resultant effect of all these efforts was the possibility of the emergence of a National theatre. One of the reasons why drama had gained so much popularity was its truthfulness to life. Drama was used not as a means of entertainment but as a means of making people aware of the reality of their own lives. The ideas presented by these dramatists were relevant not to a particular age or people but had a universal appeal. And there lies the true success of these playwrights and their plays.

The Karnataka Theatre: An Overview

Originally, Girish Karnad belongs to the Kannada theatre and has his place very secure in the history of the contemporary Kannada drama. Hence, it will be out of place to trace its growth and development here in the present context.

Kannada theatre has a rich, glorious, and ancient heritage of performatory forms particularly in the south-west of Karnataka. Popular folk forms include Yakshagana Bayalata, Sannata, Talamaddale, Puppetry, etc.

The British administration in India introduced the art of printing and publishing in the various states of the country including the State of Karnataka. It also established modern educational institutions which started functioning across the region. All these developments influenced the Kannada literature to a large extent which ultimately led to its enrichment. The period 1880-1920 was often being termed the 'Kannada Renaissance'.

Therefore, the history of the modern Kannada theatre begins around the last quarter of the 19th century. However, candid scrutiny reveals that modernity seeped into Kannada theatre even earlier in the first half of the 19th century. It was this period when Yakshagana troupes began to travel outside their traditional geographical domain. Similarly, the popular folk form Sannata, evolved by the north Karnataka started depicting the contemporary themes. It is also observed that "a Shakespearian plot had sneaked into a Yakshagana *prasanga* (script) much before Shakespeare had been translated or adapted".[4] All these folk forms possessed mutually influential relationship with the new groups emerged in Karnataka.

Marathi and Parsi theatre had a profound influence on the Kannada theatre. During the decade 1870s-80s, the Kannada troupes visited by the Marathi and Parsi theatre companies set up a new performance system. Although this new system was based on the model of the Parsi and the Marathi theatre, it simultaneously competed against them in order to evolve a Kannada identity of its own. At the same time, a new kind of drama emerged along with the successful efforts of translating and/or adapting Shakespeare and Western plays on the one hand and the Classical Sanskrit drama on the other. These culminative activities resulted in "restructuring the folk and traditional narratives and writing social drama".[5]

Surprisingly enough, the adaptations of Shakespearian and Sanskrit drama show a similar pattern. Some of the noteworthy among them are: *Ramvarma Lilavati* (*Ramavarma and Lilavati* from *Romeo and Juliet*), *Pramilarjuniya* (*Pramila and Arjuna* from *Midsummer Night's Dream*), and *Raghuvendra Rao Nataka* (*The Dreams of Raghuvendra Rao* from *Othello*).

Chandramuri Sheshagiri Rao and Basavappa Shastri translated Kalidasa's *Abhigyan Shankuntalam*. These translations are distinct from each other. In his translation, Chandramuri used traditional metres and the dialects of the north Karnataka where as Basavappa employed complex metres and diction of old Karnataka. These two diverse explorations exhibit the emergence of two traits in Karnataka theatre: a strong professional theatre and a variety of amateurish experiments.

The collaborative efforts of the Kadasiddeshwara Sangita Natak Mandali and the Mahalakshimi Prasadika Mandali resulted in the rise of Company Natak in the north Karnataka. They introduced several innovations, for example, acts were neatly divided into scenes; women were introduced to perform female roles; dynamos were used to generate electricity, etc. In 1904, A.V. Vardachar established the Ratnavali Theatrical

Company. With it, there was a change in the mode of singing and characterization. The prevalent stereotyped renderings were replaced by the new contemporary ones. These inventions were accepted by the other companies also and through them evolved the magic formula of the phenomenon known as the company theatre.

It was Gubbi Channabasaveswara Natak Sangha that had exploited this formula to its fullest. Its achievements are two-fold: (i) It became famous in Andhra Pradesh and Tamil Nadu; and (ii) It successfully utilized the novel techniques that had been introduced in the form of spectacles, special effects, folk interludes, and modes of characterization. Gubbi Natak Sangha gave such remarkable playwrights as Bellave Narhari Sastri, Kandagal Hanumantha Rao, and B. Puttaswamaiah, etc. However, the popularity was challenged by the introduction of cinema that marked the decline of theatre. "The companies started closing down during the 1930s and the 1940s and the slide accelerated in the post-independence years. Only a few managed to survive the crisis, but could never remain the popular appeal of previous decades."[6]

Amateur theatres tried their best for the survival of the theatre in general. However, it failed to organize a unified movement. It was divided into rural and urban groups. The rural groups imitated the Company Natak within their limited capacities and the urban amateurs attempted an alternative theatre of their own. The two prominent amateur troups such as the Bharata Kalottejaka Sangita Samstha of Dharwad and Amateur Dramatic Association (ADA) of Bengaluru presented 'literary plays' to their limited membership and conducted theatre festivals and competitions. They tried their best, but could not do much beyond improving upon and refining the company acting style.

However, after 1950, the amateur theatre underwent a transition. New playwrights such as T.P. Kailasam, K. Shivarama Karnath, Adya Rangacharya, Parwathavani, etc., emerged and so did many troups such as the Literary Dramatic Association of Mysore and Vasudeva Vinodini Natya Sabha of Bagalkot. T.P. Kailasam contributed much to the amateur drama in Bangalore. K. Shivarama Karnath made several experiments in the south Kannada. The stalwart Adya Rangacharya involved himself deeply in the amateur movement in the north Karnataka while Parwathavani wrote entertaining comedies. They differed widely in concepts. However, they launched a common attack on the Company Natak genre particularly, on the artificiality and anachronism. So, the amateur theatre after 1950 exhibited a definite transition from "epic to social plays, from painted curtains to suggested scenery, from rhetoric to everyday speech, and from melodrama to broad realism".[7]

The literary activities were in harmony with the recent theatrical developments. By 1920, the Navodaya (Renaissance) movement in Kannada had produced major authors. Chiefly among them were novelists and poets. But they also wrote plays, more as closet dramas than as theatre pieces. The noteworthy among them were: B.M. Sri, who tried to bring the tragic mode of the West into Kannada drama; the classicist D.R. Bedre, who invoked Indian poetics; Srinivasa who composed epic, historical and social plays but with a unique touch of realism in characterization; and Kuvempu who chiefly reworked epic plots.

Four major authors who concentrated mainly on drama and made substantial contribution were: Samsa and T.P. Kailasam from the south and Sriranga and G.B. Joshi from the north. Most of the plays of Samsa are about the kings of medieval Mysore. He used history to counter colonial rule. Kailasam's emphasis was on the contemporary reality. In his plays, he depicted the rising middle class of the old Mysore region and interrogated their 'progressiveness'. His writing exhibits his extraordinary strength for wit and farce. Sriranga, in his plays dealt with social realism. There is an indictment of the hypocrisies of the society of his days. Joshi explored the clash between tradition and modernity by capturing the shock that feudal families in the north Karnataka encountered on entering the modern age.

Karnataka theatre reached a turning point by the 1950s. Sriranga organized a series of theatre workshops. Such a kind of effort was made for the first time in Karnataka. The informal training given in such workshops to the amateur artists created a new interest and spirit in theatre.

Shivarama Karanth worked as a catalyst for the growth, development and spread of amateur theatre. He travelled to several parts of Karnataka, working with children and many groups. The festival of plays he directed in Bengaluru in 1972 proved to be a milestone in the history of Karntaka theatre.

During the 1950s, the Navya (new or modernist) movement developed in Kannada literature and its impact was also felt in drama. Even older playwrights like Sriranga and Joshi changed their style of writing. A definite shift from realism to a variety of post-realistic approaches was clearly noticeable in the dramatic works. One such vogue was that of absurdist dramas, practised by writers like Chandrashekhar Patil, N. Ratna, and Chandrakantha Kusnoor. The wave was short-lived, but it certainly brought a turning point in the mode of writing the plays and their performances. Three important playwrights appeared in that same decade are: P. Lankesh (1935-2000), Girish Karnad (1938-), and Chandrasekhar Kambar (1938-). "Together they consolidated and crystallized all the modernist issues in well-structured plays that were not only picked up by Kannada theatre but also became renowned outside Karnataka."[8]

In his short plays, Lankesh successfully used the European trend of absurd drama and the image of post-war angry young man. Karnad made his entry with the epoch-making play *Yayati* where he portrayed a struggle for existence and emergence of a 'New Woman' with such bold female characters as Chitralekha, Sharmishtha, and Devayani. Kambar, like Karnad, used history to reflect the contemporary reality.

The modern Karnataka theatre has an intimate link with its roots that is folk and classical theatre. Notable examples are found in Karnad's *Hayavadana*, Kambar's *Rishyashringa, Jokumaraswami*, etc.

The plays of Karnad, Kambar, and, Lankesh show a definite departure from the earlier methods. Using myths, folk-tales, legends, and history they dealt with the contemporary issues, while talented younger dramatists like H.S. Shiva Prakash examined the present in the light of the past. Of late, a new trend is set which appropriates any material as theatrical "text".

Now one rarely hears of a lack of original Kannada plays; instead, directors use all sorts of available texts drawing mainly from the rich repertoire of Kannada poetry and short stories, from the ninth-century poet Pampa to contemporary authors like Devanur Mahadeva and Vaidehi. The fact that many of the resulting scripts are not literary adaptions but theatrical renderings seems to have made an impact on the notion of drama in Kannada recently, redefining the concept of playwrighting.

"There is also a marked feeling that the audience is returning to theatre, after a lull when it was perceived that television had snatched spectators away."[9] The Rangashankara theatre in Bengaluru which has a well-equipped intimate stage now has become the centre of attraction for a large number of people where a fare of festivals is organized yearly. This apparently hopeful scenario kindles a spirit that the Karnataka theatre will, again, regain the glory of the bygone age.

Girish Karnad: A Short Biographical Sketch

Girish Karnad who was born in Matheran in the vicinity of Mumbai on May 19, 1938, is said to be one of the most celebrated and successful playwrights in the contemporary era. Besides being an internationally acclaimed playwright, he is a highly-talented actor, successful director and film-maker and a man of versatile genius.

Karnad graduated from the Karnataka University, Dharwad, in 1958. After graduation, he moved to Mumbai for his postgraduate studies. While in Mumbai, he got an opportunity of watching many English, Marathi, and Hindi plays. He won the much-coveted Rhodes scholarship for his B.A. at Magdalen College, Oxford University.

In 1970-72, Karnad obtained the Homi Bhabha Fellowship for his creative work in folk theatre. After leaving his job at Oxford University Press, he got himself busy with drama and films. He served as the director of the Film and Television Institute of India, Pune during 1974-75. He was awarded Padmashree in 1974 and Padmabhushan in 1992 by the Government of India. He worked as the Chairman of Karnataka Natak Academy during 1976-78. He was a visiting professor at the University of Chicago in

1987-88. And from 1988-93, he was the Chairman of the Sangeet Natak Akademi (National Academy for Performing Arts), New Delhi. In 1994, he was honoured with the Doctor of Letters by the Karnataka University, Dharwad for his valuable contribution to art, culture and literature. He was the Inaugurator of the Seventieth Marathi Sahitya Sammelan in 1997 at Ahmednagar.

Some of the selected plays of Karnad are *Yayati* (1961), *Tughlaq* (1964), *Hayavadana* (1971), *Anjumallige* (*Driven Snow*) (1977), *Hittina Hunja* (*Bali: The Sacrifice*) (1980), *Nagamandala* (1990), *Tale-Danda* (1993), *Agni Mattu Male* (*The Fire and the Rain*) (1998), and *The Dreams of Tipu Sultan* (2004), *Maduveya Album* (*Wedding Album*) (2009), *Benda Kaalu on Toast* (*Boiled Beans on Toast*) (2014). He also has written two monologues—*Broken Images* (2004) and *Flowers* (2005). At the beginning of his literary career soon after the completion of *Yayati*, Karnad wrote a one-act play, *Ma Nishada*—a radio play.

Karnad's first play *Yayati* brought him the Mysore State Award in 1962, Government of Mysore Rajyotsva Award in 1970 and Sangeet Natak Akademy Award in 1971. His second play, *Tughlaq* also received Sangeet Natak Akademy Award. His play *Hayavadana* obtained Kamala Devi Chattopadhyaya Award of the Bharatiya Natya Sangh for the Best Indian Play of the year 1972. *Nagamandala* received Karnataka Sahitya Academy Award for the best play in 1989. His another play *Tale-Danda* won him the Karnataka Natak Akademy Award for the best play of the year 1990-91, and the Karnataka Sahitya Academy Award in 1994.

Apart from his achievements as a successful playwright, he has revealed his multi-faceted creativity through his close association with the world of television and film industry. He has displayed his talent as a screen-play writer of several successful Kannada films like *Samskara, Vansh-Vriksha, Kaadu, Ondanandu Kaaladalli* and *Cheluv* and also as a famous writer of T.V. serials, and also of dialogues. He has featured in many Hindi and Kannada movies and received critical appreciation. He has played the role of *sutradhara* for several stories in the popular audio-book series for kids "Karadi Tales". He has also been the voice of A.P.J. Abdul Kalam, the former President of India in the audio-book of Kalam's autobiography *The Wings of Fire*.

Such a long and colourful journey of Girish Karnad as a playwright, director, actor, and film-maker culminated in winning the most prestigious Jnanapeeth Award in 1999. He has thus enriched the Indian cultural scene by his valuable contribution to art, literature, theatre, and the film world. The climax of his dramatic career will be the day when he wins the much-coveted Nobel Prize for literature in the near future. It will not be an exaggeration to say that his versatile genius makes one feel that long after Gurudev Tagore, the Nobel Prize for literature is waiting for Girish Karnad!

The Sources of the Karnad Drama: Myth, Folk Tale, and History

Girish Karnad is widely appreciated for his technical experiments as well as displaying a wide range of themes and subjects. Using history, myth, and folklore, Karnad realistically treats the problems of the contemporary life in allegorical or symbolic terms. He merges myth and reality, past and present; he brings in legendary and historical figures in an effort to carry his message of restructuring the present society. It is noticed that the post-independence Indian drama has made a fresh ground both technically and thematically. Using mythological stories, Karnad represented the problems of the modern man, the absurdity of life, and man's eternal struggle to achieve perfection. Like Brecht, Karnad compelled audience to respond intellectually to the action of the play and to question it rather than accept it passively.

In the realm of Indian English drama, Girish Karnad holds a prominent place as a contemporary playwright. Earlier, most of the Indian English plays produced were meant to be read and far away from the theatrical performances. But Karnad's plays make good reading and they also make an excellent theatre. He deftly makes use of myths, legends, and history in his plays to present the contemporary issues. He firmly believes that the roots of contemporary issues are deeply embedded in them. He attempts to interpret myth and history in the modern context. He is a great craftsman in whose writing we find a fine blending of genius and intuitive vision, a fertile imagination and subtle sense of wit and humour.

The term 'myth' has been interpreted variously. It is derived from the Greek word mythos which means 'fable', 'tale', 'talk', or 'speech'. In fact, myth is a much disputed term which eludes exact definition and precise categorization. Myth is a vehicle of cultural transmission. It deals with the stories and legends of the kings, the martyrs, and the historical figures of the society to which they belong. Sometimes, it decides the spiritual temper and the morals of society. It is an informing structure through which the culture of the community is explained.

In the opinion of M.H. Abrams, myth is actually a narrative of a real experience in the past, what we call myth today is not an imaginary tale, but a real life experience of the primordial society. In his book *A Glossary of Literary Terms*, he says: "A myth is a story in a mythology—a system of hereditary stories which were once believed to be true by a particular cultural group, and which served to explain (in terms of the intentions and actions of supernatural beings) why the world is as it is and things happen as they do, and to establish the rationale for social customs and observances and the sanctions for the rules by which men conduct their lives."[10]

Folktale is a story that is handed over from generation to generation orally. "Karnad senses a native psychology behind the folktales. His re-writing of myths and folktales instills unique emotional and intellectual angle to the given prototypes and thus attains a larger frame of reference—psychologically complex."[11] The plays *The Fire and the Rain* and *Yayati* are drawn from Mahabharata; *Bali: The Sacrifice* is based on a Jain myth, *Hayavadana* is based on the story from the collection of tales *Kathasagara*; *Nagamandala*, based on the Kannada folktale, has its roots in the snake stories, whereas the monologue *Flowers* is based on a folktale from the Chitradurga region in Karnataka.

History is the story of mankind in all its aspects. The term history is taken from the Greek term *historia* the meaning of which is inquiry, interview, interrogation of an eye-witness and also reports on the results of such actions. Thus, what has happened in the past is the subject of history and in addition, it is valuable for the present and future.

Karnad treats history as the story of man's life—his triumphs and failures. "History has nurtured in Karnad a dominant will for social justice, a sincere compassion for the socially oppressed and the subaltern."...(It is observed) "Karnad's acumen...lies in a mature knowledge that history is not a directly accessible unitary past with the quality of objectivity and permanence but a process by which past is constructed and invented by the subjective self-shaped by the cultural institutions—family, religion, state."[12] Karnad has used history from trans-historical perspective. In majority of his plays, he draws the sources from the Indian mythology and history.

Karnad draws all the sources for his dramatic art from the Indian mythology and history. His writing is invariably rooted in the Indian consciousness, though he adopts Western techniques to some extent to reinterpret the modern life and times. He uses tradition to question its appropriateness. Following in the footsteps of T.S. Eliot, he maintains the preservation of tradition while breaking away from it. Majority of his plays throw light on his strong historical sense, that is, realization of the pastness of the past that is outdated, and the presence of the past in the living present.

Karnad gives importance to Indian mythology and history to portray the Indian experience and character. As a gifted playwright like Shakespeare, Karnad discovers source materials from myth and history and employs them as metaphors for contemporary situations. Unlike the leading contemporary playwrights Mohan Rakesh, Badal Sircar, and Vijay Tendulkar, Karnad goes back to the past mythical, historical, and oral tales for his themes as well as characters and situations.

Karnad is one of the celebrated playwrights writing for the contemporary Indian theatre. He is greatly appreciated for his technical experiments as well as displaying a wide range of themes and subjects. With his artistic skill, he assimilates myth and reality, past and present and makes use of legendary and historical figures in the plays like *Yayati, Bali: The Sacrifice, The Fire and the Rain, Tughlaq, Tale-Danda, The Dreams of Tipu Sultan, Hayavadana, Nagamandala,* and *Flowers.* In doing so, he conveys the message of restructuring the present society on the solid basis of the new values of life. He never recapitulates the old myths and legends as they are in their conventional modes. He adds a new dimension to the original myth. To him, literature is an important part of historical process. This process is not a static one but is always in a state of flux. In this sense, Karnad seems to be very close to T.S. Eliot who advocates adherence to history and tradition. Karnad tries to challenge those ethical questions for which no ready-made answers are available, neither in the past nor in the present. He revises and changes myths and history to suit his dramatic purpose and design. He has been brought up in the environment of the folk theatre tradition and in a cultural atmosphere of the *Ramayana* and the *Mahabharata.* By exploiting myths and legends, Karnad tries to show how they are relevant to the modern times in presenting a modern man's dilemma.

Karnad's play *Yayati* (1961), originally written in Kannada, is based on a tale found in the *Mahabharata.* It is an existentialist play on the theme of responsibility. In this play, Karnad has successfully dealt with such issues as existentialism, man-woman relationship in the male-dominated society, caste, class, race, and gender consciousness, sense of alienation, complexities of expectations and responsibilities.

Karnad's women characters are always bold and assertive and always stand for their free will and independence. They represent the new women who are capable of raising the voice of protest against injustice imposed upon them. In *Yayati,* through the characters of Devayani, Sharmistha, and Chitralekha, he has projected the free and iron-willed women of society.

The plot of *Bali: The Sacrifice* is taken from the thirteenth-century Kannada epic, *Yashodhara Charite* by Janna, which in turn refers back to an unknown eleventh-century Sanskrit epic by Vadiraja. The story of the play revolves around the Jain myth of the cock of Dough. It focuses on the rift between the two ideologies: violence and non-violence. It brings out the traditional mind-set of Indian people who believe in rites and rituals and superstitious beliefs. The king in the play is the follower of the *Shakti*-cult, which permits animal sacrifice. But when the king falls in love with a Jain girl, he converts himself to Jainism which prohibits violence of any kind. Later on, his queen plays false to her spouse and betrays her marriage vows. Therefore, the king's mother asks him to sacrifice one hundred sheep. Now a follower of Jainism, the king refuses to do so. Finally, by the way of compromise, he agrees to sacrifice a batter-cock. The king compels his wife to satisfy him in the presence of Mahout. It is outright violence against his wife's psyche and the body. In the play, there is a fusion of religion and spirituality, faith and belief, aesthetic and functional attitudes, ritualistic performances and acts of conviction.

In *The Fire and the Rain*, Karnad exploits the myth of Yavakri taken from the Vanaparva of the *Mahabharata*. The play reveals the conflict between the orthodox Brahmin community and the benevolent tribal community. The former is rigid and ritualistic, whereas the latter is life-giving. The title of the play is highly symbolic. The Brahminic culture is Fire that destroys everything and the tribal culture is Rain that sustains life. By means of the two myths one that of Yavakri and the other that of Indra, Karnad throws light on the universal themes of love, jealousy, revenge, violence, futility of knowledge, weakness of human nature and loneliness.

His play *Hayavadana* is a successful experiment in the use of folk motifs. In this play, Karnad has used the ancient myth of transposed heads to depict the theme of search for identity, incompleteness, love, mind-body dichotomy, social system and social norms. The main plot in *Hayavadana* is based on a story from the *Kathasaritasagara*, an ancient collection of stories in Sanskrit and its adaptation in Thomas Mann's *The Transposed Heads*. On the surface level, it deals with the theme of eternal love triangle, that is, two men are in love with one woman. At the core of the play are three friends—Devadatta, Padmini, and Kapila. Padmini marries Devadatta, but is gradually enamoured of Kapila's strong body. Their relations get tangled. The friends kill each other. Padmini, of course, with the boon of the Goddess Kali, transposes the heads, giving Devadatta Kapila's body and vice-versa. The wrong transposition of heads creates a complicated problem of human relationship and that of identity. Thus, the myth of transposed heads portrays the human predicament in a contemporary social situation.

The play H*ayavadana* represents that no human being is complete by himself/herself. The real cause of this incompleteness is the dichotomy between mind and body. Lord Ganesha, the elephant-headed God, symbolizes this physical deformity. In the play, *Hayavadana*, the horse-headed man, represents this physical incompleteness. The *intellectuals*, in their attempts to acquire knowledge, lose their body and the *shudras*, in their efforts to grow strong through physical exercise, lose their intellect. The character of Hayavadana becomes a complete horse, when the Goddess Kali grants to fulfil his wish. His mother also feels happy, when her husband curses her to become a mare. It is the head and not the body that establishes a man's real identity. The head stands for intellectual attainments and the body for physical pleasure. What is more important between the two—the head or the body? That is the real dilemma, which forms the core of the play's story. How to resolve this dilemma of head versus body has been an enigma for centuries.

In *Nagamandala*, Karnad has used an Indian folktale and the form of story-telling in a very fascinating way. It is a folk play like *Hayavadana* based on the two oral tales from Karnataka, which he first heard from A.K. Ramanujan. The central issue of the play is Rani's fidelity to her husband, Appanna who exercises complete supremacy over his wife and himself develops an illicit relationship with a concubine. In order to win the love of her husband, she gets ready to try the love potion given to her by Kurudavva. The red colour of the blood-red potion leaves her panicky and in a moment of bewilderment she throws it off upon a nearby ant-hill. Naga drinks it and immediately falls in love with Rani. He starts visiting her at night in the form of Appanna. The love relationship results in Rani's pregnancy. Appanna, her husband, accuses her of infidelity.

Thus, *Nagamandala* represents the sexual oppression of women in the Indian society for ages. Appanna enjoys sex with a concubine openly but he seeks to punish Rani for sleeping with Naga who assumes the form of Appanna. The village elders, on the Day of Judgement, ask her to prove her chastity by giving an ordeal. At the suggestion of Naga, she successfully goes through a snake-ordeal and wins the respect of the entire village.

However, the ordeal, on the day of judgement, exposes the gender-based values, morals, and injustice of our society, which demands the loyalty of a wife to her husband but not vice-versa. In short, the play is a social satire that criticizes the society, which has oppressed women for ages and let men go scotfree to commit more sins. The characters of Appanna and Naganna (who is none else than Appana's alter-ego) symbolize a woman's exploitation and double standards of man while that of Rani symbolizes a woman's eternal endurance of this injustice. The play questions the authenticity of traditional values and conventions and in their place presents a new interpretation of a panorama, vision which imbibes the changing social reality.

The dramatic monologue *Flowers* is based on a folktale from the Chitradurga region of Karnataka which fundamentally deals with the metaphysical dilemma between *Dhárma* and *Kāma* the twin pivots of human existence.

By exploiting myths, legends, and folktales, the playwright tries to show how they are quite relevant in portraying a modern man's predicament. The use of myths and legends provides him ample scope to take up significant issues like existentialism, problems of identity, patriarchy and man-woman relationship, the motif of caste-system, pervasive sense of alienation and manifestations of human passions like love, hatred, anger, sex, sacrifice, treachery, etc.

Karnad, in some of his plays, uses history to interpret the contemporary life and its problems. There has been close association between myth and history; both narrate the past events. Actually, Karnad treats history as a battleground for the class of interests, values, and personalities. The social reformer Basavanna in *Tale-Danda*, the medieval king Tughlaq in the play *Tughlaq* and the 18th century king of Mysore, Tipu Sultan in *The Dreams of Tipu Sultan* are the historical personalities but they have gained a mythological status with the passage of time. Similarly, history is used to represent the contemporary reality. These personalities and the historical events come alive and fresh with the artistic touch of Karnad. As a matter of fact, myth and history are skillfuly interfused in literature.

Tughlaq is undoubtedly one of the greatest plays of Karnad which focuses on the dreamy as well as the tyrannical nature of Muhammad bin Tughlaq by giving exposure to his dual personality. Through the character of Tughlaq, Karnad symbolically exposes the Nehruvian idealism by dwelling on his role as a tyrant while implementing his plans. In his attempt to set up an ideal kingdom, Tughlaq becomes a king by killing his father and brother. People like Aziz try to abort his plan of reforms, but he persecutes all those who oppose him. The idea that Karnad seems to put forth through this play is that a king or a ruler, while his dream of cherishing an ideal kingdom, willy-nilly becomes a tyrant. This tyranny is the greatest obstacle in the way of his idealism as it represents his propensity for violence and destruction. The play is, thus, a critique on the drawbacks that exist in the minds of the rulers and the ruled. The character of Tughlaq, although taken from history, focuses, in the main, on the thematic concerns of the play and carries universal significance.

His play *Tale-Danda* is also termed as a historical play for the character of its protagonist Basavanna has been drawn from history. The events that constitute the framework for the play's plot-construction have been documented as historical events. And yet it is more than just a historical play. The historical events are closely linked up with social reformation. It recreates the twelfth-century socio-religious movement called "Sharanas" of Karnataka. It reveals Basavanna's fight against the inhuman caste-system and upholds the values of work-culture and community-living. Basavanna's sincere attempts to bring equality in all walks of life unfortunately end in violence. Thus, Karnad exploits history in order to expose intolerance and violence in the name of religion and throws light on the socio-political ills and evils of the present society.

The play unveils the ugly face of the caste system prevalent in the Indian society that cannot be rooted out without a bloodless revolution. Both the rulers and the ruled favour its prevalence and are prepared even to die for it. All the efforts of Basavanna to remove the barriers of caste and class come to nothing, when he performs a marriage of a *Dalit* boy with a *Brahmin* girl. The battle that is ultimately fought by the *Sharanas* against the orthodox people leads to the carnage and the plunder of their property by the royal army. The revolution, thus, proves to be a great failure at the instance of the counter-revolutionary force, resulting ultimately in the continuation of the old, status-quoist order.

His play *The Dreams of Tipu Sultan,* like the earlier plays *Tughlaq* and *Tale-Danda,* is a historical play. It is about the early days of colonialism which centres round Tipu Sultan and his dreams in the last phase of his life. Using the facts of history as his material, Karnad has vividly dramatized Tipu's struggle for freedom and independence. This play, like *Tughlaq,* is full of images and symbols which encompass various mysteries regarding the personality of Tipu Sultan.

The latest plays of Karnad such as *Wedding Album, Boiled Beans on Toast* and *Driven Snow* (still unpublished in English) constitute a running commentary on the current social order, "criticism of life", so to say, in the Arnoldian sense.

In *Wedding Album*, Karnad deals with the cultural degradation and thereby exposes the Hindu fundamentalism that claims purity of race and culture in the Indian context. He very candidly scrutinizes the hidden passions, lurking sexual desires that lie deep-rooted beneath apparent layers of cultural sophistication. The play is a scathing criticism on the Hindu rituals and institutions such as marriage and family that are considered to be the holiest of holy in the Indian set-up.

The play *Boiled Beans on Toast* is about the city of Bengaluru. It has a mythological origin. However, it is Karnad's running commentary on the current life in that city. Bengaluru is known for its massive cosmopolitan populace, its progress in IT, pleasant weather, cheap beer and heavy traffic. However, very little has been written or seen or heard about its average resident, that is, housewives, the non-IT professionals, labourers, senior citizens, the expatriates and others. This latest play by Karnad revolves round the unsung tales of ordinary Bengaluru citizens and their struggles.

Driven Snow is the only play with a non-Indian locale. It simultaneously depicts the post-colonial society in two nations: England and India. It explores the psyche of the non-resident Indians, especially of those who went to England with some aspirations in their minds and hearts. Similarly, it boldly portrays the sister-brother relationship which later develops into an illicit, nay, incestuous love relationship.

To conclude, it can be said that Karnad deftly moulds the socio-political milieu into the artistic form of his plays. His plays serve as a critique on the vices, drawbacks, and limitations of the contemporary Indian society. In addition, they express his dislike for hypocrisy, barbarism, superficiality, narrow-mindedness, corruption, duplicity, treachery, and violence. While depicting the drawbacks and vices of both an individual and society, the playwright's humanitarian approach and his commitment to human values are clearly perceptible.

GIRISH KARNAD'S FELLOW TRAVELLERS

It is observed that dramas written in regional Indian languages and their English translations have achieved a notable growth in the recent decades. In this modern era, cultural interaction has become a significant factor. In order to connect the two globes and make the foreign readers familiar with Indian tradition and culture, there is a need for English translation of literature in the Indian languages. Playwrights like Vijay Tendulkar, Girish Karnad, Badal Sircar, and Mohan Rakesh have made bold innovations and experiments. They are set out to let the new, tabooed subjects to shock the sensibility of the conventional readers. Their main object is to change the mindset of the people and make them conscious of the harsh realities of their own lives.

(a) Mohan Rakesh

Mohan Rakesh chooses the historical or semi-historical background to interpret contemporary life in most of his plays.

However, he always tries to project something that is challenging and new. The language that differs radically from the early Hindi playwrights puts him on a higher level of competence. The dialogues are natural and are potent with meaning. They express the character's mental conflict, frustration, dissatisfaction, and the resulting anger in a unique, and unusal manner.

In the play *One Day in Ashadha,* Rakesh uses history and legend to focus on the contemporary issues. The play shows that the ideal concepts such as love, devotion, commitment, sincerity, etc., are beyond one's reach or realization. A sensitive playwright like Kalidasa, who is the protagonist of the play, cannot keep himself away from royal baits or temptations. He marries the princess and betrays Mallika, his beloved, who remains a perennial source of poetic inspiration in his career as a poet.

In the play *The Great Swans of the Waves,* Rakesh depicts the dilemma of a modern man who can neither renounce life nor love it completely. Sundari represents love of life and Buddha that of renunciation of it. Being unable to make a sharp choice, Nand, the protagonist of the play, is caught in the inner conflict between mind and soul. This conflict ultimately results in lovelessness, since he can neither love life nor renounce it completely.

In his social play, a family drama, *Half Way House,* Rakesh exhibits not only men but women also perpetuating violence and exploitation in the family. Mahindranath provides everything that his wife wishes and loses all his capital in his business. At this juncture, his wife does not give him moral support. Instead, she condemns him for behaving not like a "man" with guts but like a pawn. The duality of her nature and behaviour becomes the cause of suffering for the entire family.

The play *Mad Delight* exposes the absurdity of modern life, where people just go on making adjustment and playing roles imposed on them by the socio-cultural environment of the times. In the process, they forget their real identity.

Mohan Rakesh, through his plays, depicted the mental conflict, helplessness, frustration, dissatisfaction, and anger of the modern individual who could not adjust himself with the fast-changing society. He deftly handled the problem of man-woman relationship. Kalidas in *One Day in Ashadha,* Nand in *The Great Swans of the Waves,* Mahindranath in *Half Way House* ran away from Mallika, Sundari, and Savitri, respectively. Whether the protagonists of these plays became successful in achieving their goals and whether their life-mates could brave the odds in their respective lives were the issues left for the audience's imagination and understanding of their deeds and misdeeds.

Rakesh in his plays, thus, explores "the modern man's failure to understand himself and others and their mutual failure to understand each other, which is the real tragedy of modern life".[13]

(b) Badal Sircar

Badal Sircar appeared in the Indian theatre at an appropriate time when Indian drama was at the threshold of a new era of innovation and experimentation. He introduced a new dramatic idiom in Bengal. His plays dealt with the theme of meaninglessness of our existence that led to the state of anguish and depression. The cross section of the society he chose was middle-class and the questions he handled were politico-economic, socio-cultural, and psychological ones.

His play, *Evam Indrajit,* is a classic of the contemporary Indian theatre. He firmly believes that theatre is an instrument of social transformation. His plays like *Evam Indrajit* (1962), *That Other History* (*Baki Itihas*, 1964), *There's No End* (*Shesh Nei*, 1971), and *Mad Horse* (*Pagla Ghoda*, 1967) deal with political, social, psychological and existential problems. Greatly influenced by the Russian playwright Grotowski's concept of 'Poor Theatre', Sircar formulated his 'Third Theatre' which surpasses the confines of the urban commercial theatre and the indigenous folk theatre. Putting aside all the stage props like sets, costumes, lights, sound, etc., Sircar's Third Theatre lays stress on the most important tool that is "human body". Through his Third Theatre, Sircar wants to focus on the nature of exploitation in the realm of industry and agriculture and to establish equality among people by making them aware of their existence. He wrote several plays in support of his idea of the Third Theatre, viz. *Procession* (1972), *Bhoma* (1974) *Stale News* (1979), etc. Sircar has attempted to revolutionize the Indian theatre elevating it to the Euro-American drama. The influence of Sartre and Camus is quite evident in the treatment of his themes and delineation of his characters.

Badal Sircar presents contemporary situations and social problems in his plays. His early plays express the meaninglessness of human existence that ultimately results in the state of anguish. The plays *Evam Indrajit, That Other History,* and *There's No End* are based on political, economic, social, and cultural problems. All these plays present the failure of man to get involved in the fast-changing society that leads to the sense of guilt along with resultant frustration that disturbs or discomforts the audiences and makes think a new and a fresh.

Sircar is interested in creating a theatre of his own design and writes realistic plays to fulfil his commitment to the society at large. It is his "Free Theatre", or the "People's Theatre" or the "Third Theatre". Here, he has minimized the use of sets, costumes, music, etc. The characters in his later plays, to use Sircar's own words, are "a prototype of a particular class in the society at a particular period".[14]

The most important thing about his plays is that they are free from the excesses of emotion and sentiment. In the description of the tragic characters and action, the playwright remains quite detached. So, most of his plays are perfect examples of playing sedulous ape, consciously or unconsciously, to what Brecht calls the "Epic Theatre" creating "Alienation-Effects" on its audience. The plays are intended to make the audience ponder over the dilemma of the protagonists, and in the process, they become self-aware and self-introspective.

The character of Indrajit in the play *Evam Indrajit,* represents "the angry young man" who is not satisfied with the contemporary life but can do nothing against its banality. The play ends with his realization that he is not different from others and life remains the same wherever you go. This realization leaves him hopeless and frustrated. The playwright, thus, presents a brilliant, thought-provoking play with the overtones of existentialism. According to Eakambaram, "The play is an Indian version of *Waiting for Godot*."[15]

Presenting the scenes of the Santhal Revolt in the British India, Sircar conveys through *Stale News* that social inequality, oppression, and exploitation are the inevitable features of the Indian society in all the periods of our history. The situation has changed neither in the British regime nor in free India. The incidents in the play indicate that the Indian Government is as bad as the British Government, since both of them oppress the people of the lower strata of the society and protect those of the higher strata.

The play *That Other History* describes the storm and violence caused by the demon that lives within the mind of human being, not in the outer society. It is this demon of hatred, malice and ill-will in our mind that remains responsible for war, violence, and destruction that constitute the dark side of history.

The play there's No End deals with such themes as the cruel absurdities of life, aspirations and frustrations of the urban generation, man's indifference to society that is going more and more critical and so on.

In the play *Procession,* Sircar represents the meaninglessness of human life. The so-called wonders, innovations, and development of science and technology such as the various means of entertainment, press, mass media, etc. make human life worthless. People are made mindless through nationalism, religion, education, and many other sources so that they can sustain the perpetuation of the exploitative and oppressive character of our culture.

In *Bhoma,* Sircar represents the dehumanized condition of life. Exploitation and oppression are the integral parts of it. The play communicates that you want others to love you but you yourself are not inclined to love others. The spiritual sterility depicted here is similar to that of one portrayed in *The Waste Land* by T.S. Eliot. Sircar is not happy by merely criticizing the status-quoist forces here, but finds the real cause of misery lying in the lovelessness, apathy, and indifference shown to one another.

It is observed that Sircar's focus in his plays is not on a single individual but on the entire society. That is why each of his plays is a means of socio-political propaganda and, hence, by and large, seems to lack plot and characterization but carries a message of its own.

(c) Vijay Tendulkar

Vijay Tendulkar has been the most influential dramatist and theatre personality in the whole of Marathi literary culture. Initially working as a journalist, he came across all kinds of violence and evil things in society. Tendulkar exposes various forms of violence in his plays like *The Vultures* (*Gidhade*, 1971), *Ghashiram Kotwal* (1972), *Sakharam Binder* (1972). He is the avant-garde playwright who has an unconventional attitude towards contemporary human condition. Most of his plays deal with the themes of sex, violence, and sensation. Each of his plays *Silence! The Court is in Session*, *The Vultures, Sakharam Binder,* and *Ghashiram Kotwal* is considered his *tour de force* and a specimen of Marathi theatre of anger, violence and cruelty. After the performances of these plays, the resistance that arose was a clear proof of their being new and unconventional.

Although it was with *The Vultures* that Tendulkar's name began to be associated with sex and violence, the fact had come to notice ever since the presentation of his *Silence! The Court is in Session* on the stage. Here, he had depicted these unsuccessful white-collar middle-class people who derived vicious pleasure in inflicting miseries on others. The protagonists in *Sakharam Binder* and *Ghashiram Kotwal,* on the other hand, put others to torture to seek revenge against them. *The Vultures* presented a degenerate family where family members turned into the enemies of each other for monetary gains. All the characters in this play appeared to be the victims of malice, villainy, or wickedness. Tendulkar's other plays *Kamala, Encounter in Umbugland, Kanyadan,* etc., were based on real-life incidents and presented the contemporary problems in family as well as that of in society particularly in the field of journalism, politics, etc.

The play *Manus Nawache Bet* (*An Island Called Man*) sets Vijay Tendulkar apart from the Marathi playwrights of the earlier generation. It is with the publication of this play that he is recognized as a new playwright not only of the Marathi theatre but of the Indian theatre as a whole. In most his plays, he deals with the middle-class society, in which he portrays an individual in conflict with his society. The plays explore the contemporary problems that are discussed thoroughly and at length. However, the playwright does not propose any remedy or offer any solutions. The main purpose of the dramatist is to make the people conscious of their own problems and not to find out solutions for them. Like Brecht, he is against the emotional involvement of the spectators in the action of the play. Tendulkar's plays are thought-provoking in the sense that they enable the audience to think rather than passively accept the situation that they offer. A modern man is presented with all his complexities. The dialogues are jerky and half-finished. But they signify more than what they say: For that, one needs to read between the lines, therefore!

The play *Silence! The Court is in Session* has earned him a place of honour among the leading Indian playwrights in the late sixties while *Ghashiram Kotwal* has won him an international renown in the mid-seventies.

The play *Silence! The Court is in Session* is based on a real-life incident. The stimulus comes from an amateur group on its way to stage a mock trial in a village near Mumbai. This play comes as a turning point in Tendulkar's career. It is a "play within a play" or a "play in the form of a rehearsal". In it, Tendulkar has raised several questions about love, sex, and moral values prevalent in society. To expose the hollowness of the middle-class morality and dual standards of society, he makes ample use of irony, satire, humour and pathos. The success of the play lies in its universality. The questions raised by Benare, the play's protagonist, exist in all ages and societies. Benare is projected here as a rebel against the so-called established values such as snobbery, cant and hypocrisy of a basically orthodox but sophisticated society. So, in a sense, she may be seen as Tendulkar's projection of a "New Woman" in the Indian context.

The play *The Vultures* stands apart from the other plays of Tendulkar in that it is a play, which displays the unmitigated violence arising from selfishness, greed, and sinfulness. It is explored through the depiction of an upper middle-class family sans moral values. Hari Pitale, the father of the two sons Ramakant and Umakant and a daughter Manik, prospers in his business by cheating his brother. The two sons and the daughter follow their father's treacherous ways. Ultimately, "they form a family of vultures",[16] with their victim-victimizer roles and relationship.

Sakharam Binder explores complexities of human nature. Through the character of Sakharam and those of the two women Laxmi and Champa, Tendulkar explores the depths of physical lust and violence in human being. From psychological point of view, in this realistic play, Tendulkar projects the crude perversion of individuals, caused by physical deformity in their psycho-sexual relationship. The play moves around the triangular relationship of Laxmi-Sakharam-Champa. Each of them is abnormal in his or her own way. However, they are the victims of circumstances and not of any inherent weaknesses.

The plays *Encounter in Umbugland* and *Ghashiram Kotwal*, reflect political reality and exhibit how political leaders render people mindless and thoughtless. Despite the fact that both the plays unveil the nature of the game of power politics, and reflect the political reality of India of a specific period, they differ completely from each other in terms of subject-matter and/or thematic concern. The play *Encounter in Umbugland* is a political allegory as the characters represent historical personages and the story relates the political situation of India in the late sixties and the early seventies. It also refers to the emergence of a "New Woman" and comprises, in a small way, and quite obliquely, a critique on journalism. The play *Ghashiram Kotwal* is based on a particular incident in the 18th century Peshwa regime. It is the play in which one can notice the three-fold aspect of Indian theatre, that is, the classical Sanskrit, the folk, and the modern. The context of the play is universal, for the characters like Ghashiram, Nana, and Gauri are symbolic and, hence, belong to all ages and societies. In both the plays, Tendulkar's comment on power politics can easily be noticed.

Kamala is, again, a topical play based on a real-life incident, published in a newspaper. Ashwin Sarin, the then correspondent editor of *The Indian Express* fetched a girl from a rural flesh-market and presented her at the press conference. Representing this actual incident, Tendulkar throws light on the ghastly flesh market, the exploitation of woman in her own house and that of in society, the cut-throat competition that goes on in the success-oriented contemporary generation and the egoistic hypocrisy of the young journalists.

Kanyadan is, perhaps, the most controversial of Tendulkar's plays. It deals with the psychological study of the social tensions caused by casteism in the Indian society side by side with the development of Jyoti's character from a soft-spoken and highly-cultured Brahmin girl into a hardened spouse of a dalit poet. Likewise, it focuses on the transformation in Nath's attitude. Bitter experiences of life turn the stubborn idealist into a disillusioned realist. Through this play, as revealed in the interview sought by the present author, Tendulkar represents the defeat of his own generation that tries to tread along the path of idealism.

Tendulkar's play *A Friend's Story* deals with the bold theme of lesbianism. The action of the play moves round the central character of Sumitra Dev, abbreviated as Mitra in the play. The playwright develops the character of Mitra through the comments of Bapu whose role is similar to that of *sutradhara* in a Sanskrit play or that of the chorus in a Greek play. It is based on Tendulkar's story *Mitra* which he had written in the mid-50s. The story is related to the actual life-story of a girl who lived in Pune and whom Tendulkar had seen performing a male role on the stage.

The play's subject is bold. Mitra is portrayed as one having physical hormonal imbalance. She herself is conscious of the fact that she is distinct from other girls having a stubborn nature like that of a boy—always following her instincts. She is reckless in the sense of being quite apathetic to social norms and moral values.

In all his plays, there is a variety of themes, situations and characters. Thematically, the plays range from the tragedy of a modern individual to the currents and cross-currents of the present-day politics, from the depiction of man-woman relationship to the re-interpretation of the historical episodes. Each play has a form, different from that of the previous one. Some of them are naturalistic, some are absurd, humorous and satirical, and some have the form of traditional musical folk plays. The gradual change in the theme and the structure of the play throws light on Tendulkar's creative genius in drama that remains unparalleled in the whole realm of the Indian English theatre.

To put it in short, it is observed that the main objective of these dramatists is to make people conscious of the reality of life. The dark side of life is projected in such a manner that it makes people think and feel guilty of their apathy, ignorance, and insensibility. Through all these plays, each of the playwrights in the four major Indian languages throws light on the most complex, problematic issues of the contemporary society.

Conclusion

In the pre-independence era, the Indian English drama is on decline, but in the post-independence period, the translated plays of Girish Karnad from Kannada, Vijay Tendulkar from Marathi, Badal Sircar from Bengali, and Mohan Rakesh from Hindi won them national and even international recognition. They have made bold innovations and experiments not only with the themes but with the settings, stage directions, and costumes also.

They introduced neglected, even forbidden subject-matters to shock the sensibility of the conventional audience and awaken them out of their self-complacency. The chief object of these playwrights is to transform the mind-set of the people and to bring revolutionary changes in the modes of their thinking, feeling and behaving. The playwrights' commitment to human values can be clearly perceived in their plays.

The plays produce a complex, variegated picture of a society divided against itself on the basis of gender, class, caste, etc. Inequality, corruption, and violence stigmatize the fair name of humanity. The life projected in these plays is miserable, full of contradictions, but it is wholly real.

The protagonists are sensitive, angry, and frustrated people, like most of us. This peculiar temperament of the protagonist disturbs the audience and gives them such a jerk that they are lulled out of their unconsciousness. It makes them introspective and, finally, sensitive to the issues of life. As a result, their outlook is broadened, their sensibility is sharpened, and their vision becomes clear.

It is observed that these major four playwrights have not just contributed to the respective regional drama but have given it a new dimension also. Their plays perturb the audience by raising serious, complex issues that remain unsettled even today in the contemporary society. It is the subtle and variegated nature of their plays that gives them pride of place in the international galaxy of playwrights.

In the plays of these playwrights, we have a glimpse of great Euro-American playwrights. One can still feel a superb touch of Indianness about them. The folk form that is related only to the Marathi theatre such as *tamasha* and modes of recitation and story-telling specific to the region, some trends in the Sanskrit theatre such as *nandi,* i.e. a play's beginning with a prayer to Lord Ganesha and *sutradhara,* i.e. a character that plays a role akin to that of the chorus in the Greek drama have been used effectively. So, it can be stated that the plays of these playwrights may be said to have bridged the gulf between the traditional and the modern, the native and the exotic elements that characterize our national theatre.

This study, to sum up, arrives at some significant inferences. The dramatists aim at bringing to light some of the most complex and vital issues of our existence, inner and outer. Some of the plays of these stalwarts can be looked upon as classics, as they dissolve the boundaries between the particular and the general, the temporal and the eternal, the local and the global. They are sublime and universal since the situation depicted and the characters portrayed in them go beyond time and place. The problematic issues raised in the plays belong to all times and climes. Thus, the plays are *par excellence* and are said to have set a high watermark in the field of dramataics and dramaturgy.

Notes

1. N.S. Dharan, *The Plays of Vijay Tendulkar.* New Delhi: Creative, 1999, 21.
2. *Ibid.*, 18.
3. Arundhati Banerjee, "Introduction". *Five Plays of Vijay Tendulkar*. Bombay: OUP, 1992, viii.
4. Anand Lal (Ed.). *Theatres of India: A Concise Companion.* New Delhi: OUP, 2009, 49.
5. *Ibid.*, 50.
6. *Ibid.*, 52.
7. *Ibid.*, 53.
8. *Ibid.*, 55.
9. *Ibid.*, 57.
10. M.H. Abrams, *A Glossary of Literary Terms*. Bengaluru: Prism (Reprinted), 2007, 106.
11. Vanashree Tripathi, "Introduction". *Three Plays of Girish Karnad: A Study in Poetics and Culture*. New Delhi: Prestige, 2004, 19.
12. *Ibid.*, 25.
13. N. Choudhari, "Hindi Drama". *Comparative Indian Literature.* Ed. K.M. George. Mumbai: Macmillan, 1984, 512. Quoted in Manchi Sarat Babu. *Indian Drama Today*. New Delhi: Prestige Books, 1997, 24.
14. Badal Sircar, "Azad Memorial Lectures". 1982. Cited by Ella Dutta. "Introduction". *Three Plays: Badal Sircar*. Calcutta: Seagull, 2009, 1.
15. Manchi Sarat Babu, *op. cit.*, 95.
16. *Ibid.*, 139.

MYTH PLAYS

2

Yayati: Struggle for Existence

Introduction

> Girish Karnad was only twenty-two when he attempted his interpretation in the play, *Yayati*. What makes his version of the tale so resonant, and startlingly original, is that he rejects the traditional glorification of the son's 'self-sacrifice' and, against a backdrop of lust, jealousy, and, racial tensions, foregrounds the tragic choices with which the young prince and his bride are confronted. Angry, energetic, ambitious, and strongly influenced by the tragic vision of the Existentialists, the play immediately established Karnad's reputation as a dramatist in Kannada and launched him on his celebrated career in the Indian theatre.[1]

Girish Karnad is one of the four eminent writers of the contemporary Indian drama, the other three being Vijay Tendulkar, Badal Sircar, and Mohan Rakesh. Besides being a successful playwright, he is a talented actor, director, and a film maker. He has several national and international awards to his credit for his valuable contribution to literature, culture, and art. His significant plays include *Yayati, Hayavadana, Tughlaq, Tale-Danda, Bali: The Sacrifice, Nagamandala, The Fire and the Rain,* etc. The outstanding feature of Karnad's writing is the use of myth, folktale, and history. He attempts to re-interpret the past relating it to the present in terms of relevance and examines the present in the light of the past.

Karnad's play *Yayati* (1961), originally written in Kannada, is based on a tale found in the *Mahabharata*. It is an existentialist play on the theme of responsibility. It re-interprets an ancient myth from the modern point of view. Priya Adarkar translated this play from Kannada into English in the mid-sixties. However, the final revised version of its English renderings was produced by the playwright himself in 2007. The play brought him the Mysore State Award in 1962, Government of Mysore Rajotsav Award in 1970, and Sangeet Natak Akademi Award in 1971. In this play, Karnad has successfully dealt with such issues as existentialism, man-woman relationship in the male-dominated society, caste, class, race, and gender consciousness, sense of alienation, complexities of responsibilities and expectations. According to B. Yadava Raju, "From the time of its publication, much discussion has focused upon its mythical and puranic background but not enough attention has been directed at its concern with caste, class and gender. The play has not been studied and scrutinized on such lines of understanding. Yet these concerns of class and gender illumine the characters of the play in a fascinating way and make us aware of the subliminal tensions of the drama that is enacted."[2]

The Play's Theme and Story

In the puranic tale, Yayati marries Devayani, the daughter of the great sage Sukracharya. Sharmistha, the daughter of the Asura king accompanies Devayani as her maid as per the condition laid down by Sukracharya. In the course of time, Yayati is fascinated by Sharmistha's beauty and marries her in secret. She has three sons: Druhyu, Anu and Pooru and Devayani has two sons: Yadu and Turvasu by Yayati. Very soon, Devayani discovers the secret of this marriage. In her seething anger and jealousy, she demands her father to bring a curse of decrepitude and infirmity upon Yayati. As a lascivious king, Yayati indulges in sensual pleasure. On the constant request of Yayati, Sukracharya has given a saving clause: If anybody is willing to exchange his old age, his youth will continue as before. Yayati asks the people of his kingdom and, then, in desperation, urges upon his sons to exchange their youth with his old age. All the sons except Pooru reject his demand. Pooru willingly accepts his old age. As a result, Yayati remains young, while Pooru turns into a weak and senile man. Regaining his youth, Yayati pursues pleasures with a renewed zeal and zest.

However, in the course of time, he realizes that sensual desire is never quenched by indulgence. He forsakes his life of sensual pleasures and returns the youth to Pooru and crowns him as a king at a coronation ceremony. This story is recounted in the first chapter of the *Mahabharata*.

Critical Interpretation and Appraisal of the Play

In an interview, Karnad states, "I was excited by the story of Yayati, this exchange of ages between the father and the son, which seemed to me terribly powerful and terribly modern. At the same time, I was reading a lot of Sartre and the Existentialists. The consistent harping on responsibility which the Existentialists indulge in suddenly seemed to link up with the story of Yayati."[3]

Instead of inventing a new plot, Karnad uses a pre-existing narrative and gives it a complex shape and meaning. In the present play, he adds new characters and handles the theme in such a way that it makes appeal to the contemporary times. In this connection, Seema Suneel opines, "The purpose and theme of the play are revealed through the character of the *sutradhara*. As the play opens, the *sutradhara* informs the audience that it is a mythical play—a page from the history of the unknown past. The characters, the incidents and circumstances are related to the old times. However, the reality depicted in the play is applicable to modern times as well."[4]

The play starts with Swarnalata complaining to Devayani against Sharmistha. Though Devayani defends Sharmistha, one can easily notice their tensed relationship. A sort of undeclared war is raging between them despite the fact that, once upon a time, they were bosom friends. At the base of this conflict lie the various issues of class, caste, and race. Both of them, Devayani and Sharmistha, were very conscious of their parental status and heritage. Sharmistha was the daughter of the Asura king and Devayani that of Sukracharya, the great Brahmin sage, the royal priest of the Asura kingdom. In spite of their close friendship, they were aware of the differences of their lineages.

The characters of Yayati and Pooru have unlimited freedom of choice. But the other characters of the play like Devayani,

Sharmistha, and Chitralekha cannot enjoy such a sort of freedom. Rather these women appear to be the pawns in the game played by the male characters. Therefore, they remain in the background. At the play's beginning, the *sutradhara* gives us the hint that the play is based on a mythical story of the king Yayati, and the characters and incidents of the play relate to the ancient myth in the *Mahabharata*. Nevertheless, in the hands of the playwright Karnad, they seem to go beyond time and place.

Earlier, Yayati is projected as the one who is already married to Devayani openly and to Sharmistha secretly. Later, Pooru is shown as coming back to his royal palace with his newly-wedded bride Chitralekha. Between these two parts, the exchange of youth between the father and the son takes place.

The play revolves round the myth of Yayati and the theme of existentialism as well. The nature of our existence depends upon our own choice. The famous myth of Yayati offers Karnad many possibilities of interpretation. Pooru, the son of the king, is portrayed as unheroic hero who faces terrible crisis in his life due to his own choice. Thus, the present play recounts the ancient story of a king who does not hesitate in the least to destroy his son's life for the fulfilment of his own physical desire by receiving his perennial youth and vitality. The king's motivation offers Karnad an opportunity to invent new meaning and add significance in the projection of the contemporary life and reality. The king Yayati in *Mahabharata* realizes that "fulfilment neither satisfies nor eliminates desire". "In the drama Karnad makes Yayati confront the horrifying consequences of not being able to relinquish desire, and through the other characters, he highlights the issue of class, caste and gender coiled within the web of desire."[5]

Critical Interpretation and Appraisal of the Play

In the play, the story is told with the use of a flashback technique. Yayati thinks that it is Sharmistha who pushed Devayani into the well. Sharmistha explains to him how considerate and careful she had been regarding their friendship in childhood. Despite their racial discrimination of Sura-Asura, they became the best friends of each other. One day, both of them had gone to the lake for a swim. After the swim, they lay on the bank drying their wet hair. When Sharmistha was engrossed in her thoughts about their harmonious relationship, she got disturbed by Devayani complaining that their cholis had got changed. Quite disappointedly, she told Devayani that the beautiful dream of their close friendship got shattered. Devayani remained indifferent to Sharmistha's feeling. So, she retorted her by saying: "So you were dreaming of turning into an Aryan just because you wear the choli of an Aryan woman? A famished dog gazes at the moon and believes it's a round roti" (21). Due to this unexpected venomous remark, Sharmistha was upset. She could not control herself, for in a fit of anger, she dragged Devayani by the hair and pushed her into the dry well.

Yayati was, by chance, on the way to his kingdom. In her crisis, he rescued Devayani and married her. She was the only daughter of the great sage Sukracharya. To satisfy her demand for revenge, Sukracharya forced Sharmistha, his daughter's friend and rival, to become her slave. This brings out the latent hatred and feeling of superiority in the mind of Devayani for Sharmistha. "The small quarrel grew in proportion as a complex clash of wills and, thus, began an eternal war of race, caste, and class."[6]

The tense situation that exists in the relationship of Devayani and Sharmistha is noticeable from the beginning of the play. Their arguments and counter-arguments vitiate the atmosphere of the palace. Anyone around can sense or perceive the bitterness they carry for each other. The rivalry between the two discloses their mutual distrust and anger. The playwright, indirectly, throws light on their behavioural pattern and thereby explores the class, caste, race conflict that characterizes the hierarchical Indian society in all times and climes

Although Devayani, Sharmistha, and Chitralekha are at the centre of the play's action, the society projected here is male-dominated. Through their characters, Karnad portrays strong women in society; yet they are controlled by their male-counterparts. The gender consciousness is highlighted in Yayati's treatment meted out to these women. Yayati marries

Sharmistha against Devayani's wishes. Actually, Devayani is interested in freeing Sharmistha rather than allowing her to stay in the palace. However, it is Yayati who does not allow Devayani to carry out her decision. He is so obsessed with his desire that Devayani's displeasure or anger cannot dissuade him from making love to Sharmistha. He remained very rational, practical and matter-of-fact in the matter of his marriage with Devayani. It is through Devayani that he gets an access to go close to Sukracharya from whom he intends to learn the mantra of 'mrita sanjeevani', that is, the skill of rejuvenating the dead people. Sharmistha, for the security and well-being of her race, has accepted Devayani's slavery. So, the compromise she makes, is made under social and political compulsions. Throughout the play, Karnad has shown Sharmistha as putting up the unjust, humiliating and offensive treatment not only in the matter of gender but that of her race and culture also.

Another woman character that becomes tragic in the gender-based society is Chitralekha, the newly-wedded bride of Prince Pooru. Like her husband, she too obliquely becomes a victim of Yayati's keen desire for youth and vigour. The character of Chitralekha in the drama differs from that in history. Karnad's Chitralekha is made of the stuff of a "New Woman". The king Yayati, haunted by lust and passion, cannot understand the feelings of his newly-married young daughter-in-law. It is he who sermonizes Chitralekha on the duties and responsibilities of a wife when the latter refuses to accept the transformed Prince Pooru as her husband. He expects her to behave in keeping with her status, that is, she should behave like a daughter-in-law of the Bharata family so that her sacrifice will be acknowledged with gratitude and recorded in golden letters on the pages of the dynastic history.

However, Karnad depicts Chitralekha as a bold character. She refuses to be treated like a doormat. Yayati tries to dominate her as her father-in-law and the king. But she remains adamant and refuses to be his pawn. She is one of those women who raises a voice of protest against the injustice done to her. That is why she argues with Yayati and says: "What else is there for me to do? You have your youth. Prince Pooru has his old age. Where do I fit in?" (66).

Chitralekha is portrayed as humane all through the play. She has her expectations towards her husband and life. She takes courage to ask Yayati to occupy her husband's place in her life, since he has taken away her husband's youth. So in keeping with the age-old, time-honoured tradition, she can perpetuate Bharata's lineage. Chitralekha's demand shocks Yayati who blames her for having such 'low' thoughts. But she does not succumb to the circumstances. Instead, she commits suicide and wins over her precarious life. Chitralekha's suicide is an eye-opener to Yayati, who now realizes his blunder in accepting his son Puru's youth which he returns to him. He, then, goes into the forest and lives the life of a recluse there.

Women, thus, seem to occupy unique place in Karnad's literary canon and *Yayati* is no exception to it. Through the characters of Devayani, Sharmistha, and Chitralekha, he has presented the iron-willed women in society. All of them are:

> subject in varying degrees to whims of men, but succeed in subverting the male world through an assertion of their own rights and privileges...the fictional Chitralekha adds another dimension to gender conflict, because, unlike Pooru, she rejects the king's authority over her, and sees no reason why 'my existence (should be) immolated at the altar of some empty bubble in the future' (Act IV). Before killing herself, she also reminds Yayati that incestuous adultery between them would be the logical implication of his assumption of Pooru's youth.[7]

Chitralekha is the representative of modern woman who asserts her individuality and fights for her rights. She boldly argues and directly hurls a challenge at Yayati to share matrimony with her as he has taken away her husband's youth. Karnad's Sharmistha is quite distinct from that of the *Mahabharata*. It is not she who is interested in Yayati but it is Yayati who gets bewitched by her physical charms. She is practical-minded and is guided by reason. That is why she tries to dissuade Pooru from accepting his father's old age, since she says: "No, no, no, you can't. It is utter stupidity! Pooru, the desire for self-sacrifice is a rank perversion" (50). According to Aparna Dharwadker, "This chorus of unusual female voices, mixed in with the flawed male utterances, humanizes the myth and gives it ethical and dialectical weight."[8]

Now, let us study and examine Swarnalatha's episode and draw our conclusion from it:

> Swarnalatha, the maid of Devayani was the only child of her parents. They arrange a boy who taught her to read and write properly. As she grew young, she was married to a suitable boy. They lived happily. But when her husband came to know about her coaching by a Brahmin boy, he got suspicious and started torturing her. Swarnalatha could not prove her innocence. For her husband's satisfaction, she tells him a lie that the Brahmin boy had indeed violated her. Her husband was rid of his dilemma but the very next morning, he left the house once and for ever. "Swarnalatha's narrative once again emphasizes the patriarchal norms of the society that expects a woman to prove her innocence. She is never taken on her own worth."[9]

The society, therefore, projected here is a male-dominated one. It expects a woman to be loyal to her male-companion, to follow his will without any protest or in due obedience to his word as law. The fact is borne out by the play's structure, its plot and sub-plots.

Here is brief note on the play's existentialism: Karnad had written the play when he was about to leave India for England. His parents were deadly against his decision thinking that he would settle there. During this period of emotional turmoil, he read the *Mahabharata*. The story of *Yayati* caught his attention and the ultimate result was the creation of the play. However, it is not a mythical or historical play. Using the incident in ancient Indian history, Karnad here projects modern man's dilemma who cannot make a proper choice and therefore turns out to be tragic. R.K. Dhawan opines: "...the theme of the play was taken from ancient Indian mythology. While the theme was typically native, the play owed its form, not to numerous mythological plays he watched, but to western playwrights whom he had read. While the subject-matter was purely native and traditional, the form and structure were essentially western."[10]

Although the play is based on a traditional tale, Karnad has given it a new meaning and significance highly relevant in the context of contemporary life. The beginning and the end of the play is similar to that of the story in the *Mahabharata*. Karnad's originality lies in working out the motivations behind Yayati's ultimate choice. The story in the *Mahabharata* ends with Yayati's realization that desire does not come to an end with its fulfilment. So, he returns Pooru's youth. However, Yayati in Karnad's play recognizes the horror of his new life, and accepts the moral responsibility of his own choice and, therefore, returns the youth to Pooru. So, the play is existential in nature. In his essay "Existentialism and Humanism", Sartre states:

> To be is to live. To live is to act and to act is to choose and to choose is to invent values and to invent values is to be responsible and to be responsible is to be moral.[11]

The theory of existentialism indicates that man is a unique and isolated individual in this meaningless or hostile world. He is free to make choice. Therefore, he is responsible for his destiny. Man's life starts and ends in nothingness. The only thing man can be certain about is his existence and the course of his existence depends upon his own choice. The central principle of this philosophy is: "Existence precedes essence ... Man first of all exists, encounters himself afterwards.... Man is nothing else but what he makes of himself."[12] Thus, the existentialist philosophy makes him aware of his responsibility and ultimately leads him towards new moral consciousness. This is what happens to Yayati towards the end of the play.

The play is about adults: the elder generation that expects too much of the younger generation and thereby spoiling their future prospects. The King Yayati, just to fulfil his lust, demands of his son to sacrifice of his youth. He does not stop to ponder over what will happen to him and his family in the future. According to the young budding playwright, looking back at that point, it seemed to Karnad very significant that this was what was happening to him, his parents demanding that he should move in particular way, even when his future seemed to be opening up a new channel of development. So, it was the play where the myth in some ways gave exact expression to what he was trying to say.[13] The play is autobiographical as it reflects the playwright's anxieties, his resentment with all those kith and kin, who seemed to demand, in sheer love, of him the sacrifice of his future.

The roles of the characters are so altered as to fit into the framework of existentialism. In the original myth, Pooru is portrayed as an obedient son who sacrifices his youth for the sake of his father. He has no identity of his own. Karnad rejects the traditional glorification of the son's self-sacrifice. In the play, Pooru seems to be caught in the existential dilemma. He is alienated and finds his own role incomprehensible and is, thus, reduced to a pathetic figure. With no faith in tradition, nor any aim in life, he accepts his father's curse without consulting his newly-wedded wife. Aparna Dharwadker opines:

> Pooru is a philosophical but self-hating 'outsider' who feels unsettled by the questionable legitimacy of his birth, and oppressed by the weight of dynastic tradition. When the curse is pronounced, Pooru accepts it, because he thinks the sacrifice of his youth would counteract his feelings of unworthiness, and enable him to fulfil his destiny as a Chandravamsha Prince.[14]

Thus, the play seems to end on an existential note. Through the myth, Karnad seems to convey the idea that man himself is responsible for his destiny. Yayati emerges as a tragic character, since he cannot take proper decision. He himself is responsible for his degradation. His refusal to part with Sharmistha is the real cause of his tragedy. It is the pathetic end of Chitralekha that brings him to his senses and forces him to repent for his moral transgression. He cannot bear the disastrous effect of his action and finally takes back the curse from his son.

Conclusion

Thus, to sum up the discussion in the words of Nand Kumar, it can be stated: "Karnad's *Yayati* successfully conveys his message of performance of duty and acceptance of responsibility. He seems to have used the myth of Yayati with a view to exposing the absurdity of life with all its elemental passions and conflicts. His Yayati, on the other hand, rejects passionate attachment to sensual pleasure to which the king is a slave and pleads for a life of responsibilities and self-sacrifice as represented by Pooru in the play."[15] The play is concluded with Yayati's words; "Take back your youth, Pooru. Rule well. Let me go and face my destiny in the wilds" (69).

Like a Sanskrit play, Yayati ends on a happy note with an announcement made by the *sutradhara* that "Pooru ruled long and wisely and was hailed as a philosopher-king" (70).

Notes

1. Girish Karnad, *Yayati*. New Delhi: OUP, 2008, jacket of the book.
2. B. Yadava Raju, "Race and Gender in *Yayati*". *Girish Karnad's Plays: Performance and Critical Perspectives*. Ed. Tutun Mukherjee. New Delhi: Pencraft International, 2006, 80.
3. Seema Suneel, "Girish Karnad's *Yayati* Reconsidered". *New Directions in Indian Drama*. Eds. Sudhakar Pandey and Freya Barua. New Delhi: Prestige, 1994, 126.
4. *Ibid.*
5. B. Yadava Raju, *op. cit.*, 81.
6. *Ibid.*, 83.
7. Aparna Dharwadker, "Introduction". *Collected Plays: Girish Karnad*. Vol. 1, New Delhi: OUP, 2005, xvi-xvii.
8. *Ibid.*, xvii.
9. B. Yadava Raju, *op. cit.*, 86.
10. R.K. Dhawan, "Girish Karnad: The Man and the Writer". *The Plays of Girish Karnad: Critical Perspectives*. Ed. Jaydipsingh Dodiya. New Delhi: Prestige, 1999, 15.
11. Sharad Asolkar, "Astitwawad ani Sartre". *Yugwani*. Ed. Sharad Kolarkar. May 1980, 19.

12. *Ibid.*, 18.
13. Girish Karnad, "Acrobating between the Traditional and the Modern". *Indian Literature*. Vol. xxxii. No. 3, May-June 1989, 90.
14. Aparna Dharwadker, "Introduction". *op. cit.*, xvi.
15. Nand Kumar, *Indian English Drama: A Study in Myths*. New Delhi: Sarup & Sons, 2003, 122.

3

Bali: The Sacrifice: Violence: Actual and Imagined

Introduction

The first version of *Bali: The Sacrifice* was published in Kannada under the title—*Hittina Hunja* in 1980 and was performed in both Kannada and Hindi. However, Karnad re-edited the play in English, when he was commissioned by the Leicester Haymarket Theatre, England to write for them. This English version was performed at the theatre in 2002 and was published in 2004 along with *The Dreams of Tipu Sultan* by the OUP.

The plot of this play is taken from the thirteenth-century Kannada epic *Yashodhara Charite* by Janna which in turn refers back to the ninth-century Sanskrit epic *Yashastilaka* by Somadeva Suri. The story of the play revolves round the Jain myth of the cock of dough. The play is strewn with religious tensions and discussions on the dynamics of psycho-sexuality. Karnad, very artistically, juxtaposes the sexual issue with the psycho-religious tensions born of violence. The king, in the play, is a follower of the *Shakti*-cult which permits animal sacrifice. When the Hindu Kshatriya king falls in love with a Jain girl, he converts himself to Jainism which prohibits violence of any kind. But the king is devastated to discover that his queen is involved with the mahout, an elephant-keeper of his palace. In order to avert the evil consequences of her infidelity, the king's mother asks him to sacrifice a hundred sheep. But he is a Jain by conversion, and non-violence is the basic tenet of the Jain-faith. Finally, as a compromise, it is decided to substitute a cock made of dough. The king compels his wife to join him in the symbolic sacrifice and also forces her to satisfy him in the temple in the presence of the mahout. It is an act of downright violence against his wife's mind and body. Expressing her views on the thematic issues of the play and the intrinsic tendency of the king, Aparna Dharwadker rightly observes: "The central 'problem' in the play is, thus, not the queen's adultery but the deep spiritual rift between...Jainism—and the traditional Kshatriya ethos of her husband's family...."[1]

In *Bali: The Sacrifice*, along with the major issue of violence versus non-violence, Karnad has dwelt upon several problems of love, sex, morality, superstition, etc. prevalent in the contemporary society. All the characters in the play are used as symbols and they represent their own points of view. S. Subhas Chandran rightly remarks: "Karnad introduces a discourse on 'violence' to unsettle the moral complacency of societal orthodoxies by dramatizing the case of a queen's adultery and the subsequent chain of reactions."[2]

The Play's Theme and Story

The play has a very simple plot. It consists of just three actions: queen's adultery with the mahout, mother's queen's demand to perform the ritual of sacrifice and the queen's sacrifice for the principles of her Jain religion.

The play starts with the queen's song. When the curtain rises, the inner sanctum of a ruined temple is noticed. As the play begins, the stage is dark. The two indistinct figures inside the sanctum: the mahout and the queen are displayed sitting apart from each other. The king is noticed sitting on the outer steps of the temple with a torch in his hand. Through the dialogues, the queen's adultery with Ashatavakra, the palace mahout is revealed. The heavenly voice of the mahout has lured the queen out of her bed and has brought her to the singer in the deserted temple.

The queen is neither curious about the mahout nor is she inclined to disclose her identity. Actually, she is trying to escape from the situation to keep the incident secret. The mahout is clever enough to guess that she must be from the upper class of society. To extend her stay, he narrates to her the story of his birth. The king sits on the outer steps of the temple. The two in the inner sanctum are unaware of his presence. Later on, both the queen and the mahout notice some movement in the courtyard. Hearing the knock at the temple gate, they are greatly terrified. In order to drive out the strangers standing outside, the mahout produces sounds of love-making. At last, the king comes into the temple with a torch in his hand searching for the queen. He calls out and the queen presents herself before him. The mahout is stunned to know that the woman with whom he was making love is none other than the queen herself.

The queen is least guilt-conscious. She informs the king that she is being seduced by the music even before submitting to a physical association. She quite frankly tells him: "I was sleeping by your side. His singing woke me up. The song... (he) caressed me, enveloped me.... For a brief moment, nothing mattered. The palace. Me. You. Only the song. I felt like a flame burning bright. Pure. When I came to my senses, I was here. By his side" (119).

The mother queen is suspicious of her daughter-in-law's fidelity and, therefore, asks the king about the temple incident. Due to the constant persuasion of mother about his distraught state, the king answers her: "...I had a dream. It woke me up. ...in the dream...I saw that the royal swan in our garden had got caught in mud..." (103).

More penetrating questions of the mother queen compel the king to reveal the fact. The disclosure of the direct, the false move makes her violent. She displays her horror and demands of him to perform the sacrifice of a hundred sheep to her goddess to acquit the queen of her sinful act, which is bound to have its adverse impact upon the well-being of her son and the kingdom. Being a Jain now, the king refuses to perform the act of violence. So, the mother, by way of compromise, suggests to him to offer the substitute, that is, the cock of dough. The queen exhibits her intense disliking for her mother-in-law's conventional ways of propitiating gods and goddesses. That is why she refuses to join in performing the ritual sacrifice of the artificial cock made of dough as demanded by her mother-in-law. However, her love and loyalty to her husband make her to participate in the symbolic sacrifice. She says, "I am making you suffer. We are here. I love you. I don't want you to suffer. I agree to the sacrifice" (239). When she joins the king to pierce the sword into the cock, she imagines that the cock of dough begins to crow. She gets horrified. The king tries to cool her down. But a cock crows outside. So, the king turns to the door. The queen drives the point of the blade into her womb and falls on the sword. At last, at the point of death, she falls into the king's arms. Making compromise with her principles hurts her heart and the staunch upholder of non-violence ends her life in suicide, that is, by resorting to violent means.

Though the play has a little dramatic action, the playwright throws light on the past life of the characters through the flash-back technique. In this connection, S. Subhash Chandran says: "Though the play's present has only the denouement of the Queen's action to be dramatized, the playwright provides the history of the King and the Queen from the day of their first meeting and child-marriage till the night of the adultery with the help of an expository dialogue and two flashback scenes."[3] The childhood friendship culminates into a married life. When they get married, he has been a prince of twelve and she has been the princess of eight. He is the Kshatriya and she is the Jain. Their deities are also different. Actually, they are the true contrasts of each other: his goddess, clothed in silk robes, is thirsty for blood and hers is the naked Jineswara who could never hurt a living being. The king, in accordance with the condition of the queen for marriage besides his love for her, adopts Jainism. Naturally, he follows the principle of non-violence. This conversion creates hurdles for him in two ways: His mother accuses him of forsaking his religion for the love of a woman. Similarly, it is not easy for him to forget his Kshatriya antecedents. Although he tries his best to accept the path of non-violence, the culture of Kshatriya practices always remains submerged in his subconscious.

Conjugal life proves somewhat difficult for both of them. They remain childless even after completing fifteen years of married life. The young couple is always under tremendous psychological pressure to produce an heir to fulfil their duty to the kingdom. Their love for each other gives them strength to face the moments of humiliation and pain. While facing insults and hostility from others, especially after her miscarriages, they stand together and survive external onslaughts. Subhash Chandran rightly observes: "The ruthless scrutiny about her inability to bear a child may have pushed her to a breaking point. Continuance in the similar manner would easily have led them to old age and peaceful death. But discontent and disharmony lurk beneath the surface of their seeming conjugal 'bliss' and the thin layer of make-believe 'harmony and affection' is vulnerable to pressure."[4]

Critical Interpretation and Appraisal of the Play

The main thesis of the play is developed with the help of the four characters: the two women characters, namely the queen and the mother queen, and the two male characters—the king and the mahout.

The women characters in Karnad's plays are very bold and dominating. Symbolically, they are the representatives of "new women" in society. Instead of being dictated by their men, they dictate them and compel them to follow their decisions. The two women characters in the play, the queen and mother queen best exemplify Karnad's new women. The action of the play revolves round these two women characters: the former represents Jainism, that stands for non-violence and the latter Kshatriya *dharma* that stands for violence.

The play starts with two songs—the first one sung by the queen and the second by the king. Both the songs are meaningful and suggestive for the development of the main argument of the play. The queen sings: "As the world is divided into two orbs: one lit up by the sun, the other hid in the shade, so also the human soul, the habitation of gods, is split into two realms" (189).

The two orbs of the world refer to the two sections of the human souls—dark (evil instincts) and bright (good instincts). The king's song depicts his mental agony and helplessness and also throws light on the further development of the action in the play. "...But/ woe betide the times/ where the King sits alone/ outside on the steps/ racked by sighs/ while the Queen is trapped/ in her lover's thighs" (190). Here, the king himself plays the role of a *sutradhara* and unfolds the story of the play. The power of music brings the queen to the temple where she both physically and emotionally surrenders herself to the singer. In this union, she experiences the ecstasy of love. Everything happened so spontaneously that she did not hesitate to think what would be the repercussions of her action. The low-born status and ugly figure of the mahout do not become the hindrances to their mating. Quite frankly, she tells him the purpose of her visit: "Your looks don't matter to me. I came here, because I heard you sing. You have heavenly voice" (194). In spite of the repeated requests of the mahout, she remains reluctant to disclose her identity. She tries to keep her private life and public life intact. Although she enjoys the ecstasy of love with the mahout, mentally she is faithful to her husband. When the mahout proudly tells her that he is better than the king in love-making, she bluntly tells him. "My coming here has nothing to do with my husband. He is a marvellous person—affectionate, gentle, trusting" (195).

The queen's association with the unknown person raises conservative eyebrows. The play defies the matrimonial norms of Indian culture that a woman should be loyal to her husband and, therefore, has to keep herself away from any kind of illicit, sexual attraction. The king's virility is dubious and hinted at so several times in the play. It can be noticed that she has been criticized for not having a son for fifteen years. The queen mother constantly expects from her a son, an heir to the dynasty. Ignoring the established norms of society, she responds to the call of her heart. She gets what she desires. The bonds of conventional morality and the codes of fidelity are swept away by the pull of the flesh. Through the character of the Queen Amritmati, Karnad has portrayed a bold, new woman who unhesitatingly confesses to her extramarital relationship and plainly admits that whatever happened was very 'beautiful' and charming. Karnad here seems to give a message that purity that is guiltlessness of mind matters more than that of physical relationship even in the case of adultery. Neither the queen feels guilt-conscious and considers it a sinful act nor does the king blame her for it, outwardly or inwardly, out of their mutual love for each other.

In the introduction to the play, Aparna Dharwadker states: "In *Bali,* the queen is childless, and although this lack is an inescapable point of reference in her life, it is not (at least for her) a source of obsessive guilt or shame. Aroused by the Mahout's song, she seeks him out for an anonymous coupling that violates the boundaries of caste and class, but when challenged, refuses to profess guilt for her action or to atone for it through the propitiatory ritual. More than any other female character in Karnad's drama, she is transgressive presence, deprived of conventional feminine roles by chance and circumstance, but self-possessed and cerebral enough not to surrender to the presence of conformity."[5]

The union of the queen with the mahout results in her pregnancy. Both, the queen and the king are highly delighted. However, the queen mother expresses her happiness cautiously, for she has some reservations in her mind. The queen's pregnancy establishes her fertility and the king's impotency.

The character of the queen is depicted with utmost care. It symbolizes the image of a 'New Woman'. Ignoring the social norms, she follows the dictates of her mind and heart. She does not feel guilty or even ashamed of her extra-marital relationship with the mahout. She is a sincere practitioner of Jainism and takes pride in her creed. She has no faith in the existence of God and believes in the principle of love, compassion, and non-violence. She makes a compromise to satisfy her husband by joining the ritual but is not happy about it, for she owes allegiance to her religion alone. She refuses to play false to it; that is why she commits suicide. Apparently, for all others, it is suicide but for the queen it is the sacrifice that she performs on the altar of her faith. She is, thus, an example of woman's honesty and integrity and attains martyrdom for the cause of her religion. Sumita Roy comments: "Sacrifice in the true sense would mean reaching towards nothingness, not by depriving oneself but by willing renunciation which is followed through with total conviction.... Here sacrifice and surrender are seen as synonymous and the Queen uses it to 'sum up' her life, from her subjective point of view."[6]

From the traditional or conservative point of view, there is something paradoxical on the part of the queen here. On the one hand, she talks about love, compassion and non-violence and on the other, tortures her husband mentally by imposing her own will on him. She defiles the inner sanctum of the temple by having sex with the mahout. Thus, she commits the sin of sacrilege. She is extremely good-looking and thereby conquers the world by her bewitching beauty. The king is so enmeshed by her love that her illicit relationship does not affect him in the least. But such a type of criticism cannot go uncontested, for the queen's serenity of mind is juxtaposed with her adultery—to establish a woman's privilege to motherhood. Actually, the queen appears to be the mouthpiece of the playwright.

Through the contrasting characters of the mother queen and queen (since they are foils to each other), Karnad represents the age-old conflict between violence and non-violence, respectively. Aparna Dharwadker is justified, when she states: "More broadly, the Jain-Hindu debate of the pre-modern period casts an ironic light on the endemic violence of the postcolonial present in India—a problem addressed directly in both *Tughlaq* and *Tale-Danda*."[7] The message of the play may be summed up thus: Intended violence is as offensive as actual violence and the adultery committed on the mental plane is equivalent to that committed on the physical plane.

The play deals with the psychological study of the two warring women representing their own religious creeds. The play, as the title suggests, centres around the theme of sacrifice. The queen mother seems to be a very imposing character in the play. She exerts tremendous influence on her son. Since the king's conversion to Jainism shocks her to a great extent, she criticizes him saying: "You were not born a Jain. You were born my son. But you betrayed me and my faith" (214). She strongly believes in rites and rituals, gods and goddesses. She honestly feels that the bad effects of evil spirits are eliminated by performing the ritual. As a mother-in-law, she always wishes to have a grandson as an heir to the dynasty. However, the news of her daughter-in-law's pregnancy does not please her, since it gives her the awareness of the impotency of her son. She makes fun of the Jain philosophy of non-violence. What she wants to tell her daughter-in-law is that shedding of blood is necessary while giving birth to a child; without some kind of violence, life is not possible. She considers her daughter-in-law's relationship with the mahout as an illicit one and, therefore, disastrous to the royal family. In order to avoid the evil consequences which the family would face in the aftermath, she asks her son to sacrifice a hundred sheep in the ritual. When the king shows his reluctance to it, she suggests to him an alternative, i.e. offering of a cock of dough. Her constant persuasion to purify the queen by performing the symbolic sacrifice at least becomes the cause of a ruffle in the king's familial life. Through the character of the queen mother, Karnad represents the conventional mother-in-law of the orthodox Indian society, for whom the personal ego is more important than the marital bliss of her son's life. In this connection, Aparna Dharwadker observes: "What alienates her from the barren and unfaithful queen is not only a mother's possessiveness and anger, but fundamental differences of belief that insert larger cultural questions into their personal antagonism.... The familiar narrative of the two women vying for the upper hand in relation to a man becomes in *Bali*, a destructive dance in which there are no winners, only losers."[8]

The king is the central character in the play. Originally, he belongs to the Kshatriya community but after marriage, he converts himself to Jainism. The childhood friendship of the prince and the princess develops into a marital partnership and the king accepts the Jain religion for the sake of his sweet heart. The queen describes him as "a marvellous person—affectionate, gentle, trusting" (195). He seems to be rather weak and passive in comparison with the other characters in the play. He is emotionally attached to both his mother and his wife as well. Therefore, his personality is overshadowed by those of the two women. He is always swayed away by the vagaries of their desires, whims and fancies. Very helplessly he tells his wife: "I can't bring myself another mother. She can't get herself another son.... I won't look for another wife" (211). The king, due to his hesitancy and the consequent divided mind, is unable to take his own decisions. Crushed under the two strong-willed, rather obstinate women and heated verbal exchanges on their respective creeds, his life gets ruffled. Consequently, he becomes miserable a sad picture of himself.

The male characters in the play are foils to each other. The mahout represents the practical side of life whereas the king represents the mediating force between the two warring women and their ideologies. The mahout is a low-born elephant-keeper. He is aware of his ugliness and very often talks about his physical deformity. Though low-born, he knows his importance to the royal family. He is conscious of caste/class conflict in the society. He is a self-seeking opportunist. Through him, Karnad brings to light the role of physical lust in man's nature. To have sex with women is his regular practice. Quite frankly he tells the queen that he has already enjoyed sex with six women and she is the seventh one. It is noticed that he is not at all concerned with social norms or cultural values. He is interested neither in the philosophical deliberations nor in the concept of sin. He makes fun of rites, rituals and outdated practices. While speaking about the characterization in the play, Aparna Dharwadker states: "The two male characters in the play, in contrast, are arranged in relations of perfect antithesis and hierarchical reversal: the cultivated, sensitive, and valiant but impotent king versus the crude, amoral, and cowardly but potent Mahout with his irresistible song...the radical disparities between the Mahout and the royal couple underscore not an egalitarian message about the union of a queen and her servant, but the eventual irrelevance of that act to the long-term disequilibrium of the royal marriage."[9]

The other important themes of the play are the conflict between the mother-in-law and the daughter-in-law and the futility of blind beliefs and outdated ritual practices. The dispute between the mother-in-law and daughter-in-law is presented in glaring light. When the Queen Mother discovers her daughter-in-law's treachery, she reacts furiously and asks her son to "throw her bones to the dogs. She has betrayed you..." (223). Through the character of the queen mother, Karnad has portrayed the mother-in-law of the orthodox Indian society, who always intervenes in the affairs of her daughter-in-law.

Through the mythical story, Karnad represents the issues of the contemporary society. Symbolically, the characters in the play are like men and women encountered in our day-to-day lives. Although the king does not lay any blame on the shoulders of his wife, he is greatly shocked to see his wife in the arms of the elephant keeper. The queen describes the king as a marvellous, loving and caring husband but he shows his hatred and jealousy for the mahout and for his wife by humiliating her in the temple in the presence of the mahout. The king forgets the fact that the real conjugal relationship is not only based on high ideals but also on the mutual union of the mind and the body. He fails to recognize the biological necessity of his wife. He adheres to the established norms in the patriarchal society which are always one-sided, never taking into cognizance the true desire of a woman.

Thus, the characters portrayed and the situations depicted go beyond time and place. In the portrayal of his characters, Karnad remains a detached, dispassionate observer. Each character in the play is the combination of strength and weakness, good and bad. The king first appears to be loving and caring but later on turns out to be ruthless, contemptuous and revengeful but remains totally passive, confused, and dominated by the two stubborn, warring women. The queen seems to be defiant, aggressive, adamant, and a staunch follower of Jainism but her love for her husband compels her to make compromise with her cherished principles. The queen mother is also very adamant, superstitious, a hard-core believer in the tradition and is always engrossed in propitiating her goddess with rites, rituals, and sacrifices. However, she appears quite helpless, when the king marries against her wish and also adopts Jainism. The mahout is an opportunist, completely practical minded with no regret or repentance for his actions, straightforward and critical of the people belonging to the upper class of society.

The play deals with a debate on violence and non-violence which is deftly interlinked with man-woman relationship and thereby exposes meaninglessness and hollowness of courtly life. It relentlessly throws light on the futility of observing superstitious beliefs and outdated practices for they bring no solution to the problem presented in the play. The dramatist aims at bringing to light some of the most complex and vital issues of our existence. "In the Preface, Karnad describes violence as 'the central topic of debate in the history of Indian civilization'—a debate in which Hinduism has been ranged against Buddhism on the one hand and Jainism on the other. Karnad also chooses to address not the public and political carnage of war and conquest (which led, for instance, to the emperor Ashoka's conversion to Buddhism), but the legitimization of violence in ritual practices that individuals (such as the Queen Mother) regard as private acts of faith and worship."[10] To quote Dharwadker again, "The central 'problem' in the play is thus not the Queen's adultery but the deep spiritual rift between her Jainism and the traditional Kshatriya ethos of her husband's family. The King has embraced Jainism in principle, but his instinctive propensity for violence is evident in every scene,... When he compels the Queen to join him in the symbolic sacrifice so that his desire for atonement may be satisfied, her imagination breathes life into the sacrificial object and leads to her own death."[11]

Karnad shows his protest against the established conventional norms and values. He suggests that society should be reconstructed on the basis of a new code of conduct and morality. The title *Bali: The Sacrifice* signifies paradoxical connotations. The true meaning of sacrifice implies renunciation of one's own happiness or cherished principles for the well-being of the persons concerned or for the preservation of eternal values of life.

Conclusion

Thus, to sum up, we see that the play *Bali: The Sacrifice* has multiplicity of themes such as man-woman relationship, women's position in male-dominated society, violence and non-violence, love and sex, tradition versus modernity, hatred, treachery, superstition, etc. The essential feature of Karnad's plays is that they present a perplexing, distressing and complex situation in all seriousness and manifest his strong dissatisfaction with the existing social order and *Bali: The Sacrifice* is no exception to it.

Notes

1. Aparna Bhargava Dharwadker, "Introduction". Girish Karnad. *Collected Plays*. Volume one. New Delhi: OUP, 2005, xxxv.
2. Subhash S. Chandran, "*Bali: The Sacrifice* and Dionysian Life Assertion". *Girish Karnad's Plays: Performance and Critical Perspectives*. Ed. Tutun Mukherjee. Delhi: Pencraft International, 2006, 294.
3. *Ibid*., 297.
4. *Ibid*.
5. Aparna Dharwadker, *op. cit*., xxxiv.
6. Sumita Roy, "Negotiating Ideological Spaces: Reading *Bali: The Sacrifice*". *Girish Karnad's Plays: Performance and Critical Perspectives*. *op. cit*., 290.
7. Aparna Dharwadker, *op. cit*., xxxv.
8. *Ibid*., xxxiv.
9. *Ibid*., xxxiv-xxxv.
10. Girish Karnad, *Two Plays by Girish Karnad; The Dreams of Tipu Sultan, Bali: The Sacrifice*. New Delhi: OUP, 2004, 69. Quoted in Aparna Dharwadker, *op. cit*., xxxv.
11. Aparna Dharwadker, *op. cit*., xxxv.

4

The Fire and the Rain: A Rhetoric of Revenge

Introduction

The play *The Fire and the Rain* (*Agni Mattu Male*) was originally written in Kannada in 1995. It was published in English in 1998 by the playwright himself. It was successfully staged in Kannada, Hindi, and English. Many theatre critics have highly appreciated the theme and the subject-matter of the play. It stands apart from the other plays of Karnad, since it displays the unmitigated violence arising from selfishness, greed, and sinfulness. Bhaskar Chandavarkar has described the play as "not only Karnad's best work but one that he will be unable to surpass".[1] "It is a dense, intellectually ambitious, autumnal play structured around ideas...and a plethora of tangled relationships which unfold with a rare economy and intensity of words and emotions...in it, Karnad reimagines the world of Hindu antiquity and constructs a story of passion, loss, and sacrifice in the contexts of the Vedic ritual, spiritual discipline (*tapasya*), social and ethical differences between human agents, and interrelated forms of performance still close to their moments of origin."[2]

The entire play depicts the negative impulses of a human being such as anger, violence, bloodshed, jealousy, pride, false knowledge, the intense feeling of hostility, hatred, greed, treachery and revenge. Karnad finds the myth quite relevant to the contemporary society. The play communicates the message that abuse of knowledge ultimately leads to the destruction of the world. It vividly portrays the conflict between the orthodox Brahminic community and the benevolent tribal community. The former is rigid and ritualistic (symbolized by "fire"), whereas the latter is community-oriented and life-giving (symbolized by "rain"). The title of the play is symbolic and is used aptly and suggestively, exposing the play's thematic structure. The Brahminic culture is fire which destroys everything and the tribal culture is rain which bears and sustains life.

The Play's Source: The Myth of Yavakri

The Fire and the Rain is Karnad's most complex play, which is based on the myth of Yavakrita taken from the Chapters 135-138 of the Vana Parva (the forest canto) of the *Mahabharata*. The playwright spent nearly thirty-seven years to complete the play. In his note on *The Fire and the Rain*, he relates in brief, the original myth of Yavakri:

> There were two sages, Bharadwaja and Raibhya, who were good friends. Raibhya was a learned man who lived with his two sons, while Bharadwaja concentrated on his ascetic practices. Yavakri, Bharadwaja's son, nursed a grievance against the world, for he felt his father did not receive the respect and recognition he deserved.

He further went off to the forest and did *tapasya* (penance) so that he could obtain the knowledge of the Vedas direct from the gods. The rigours of his ascetic practice were such that Indra, the lord of gods, appeared to him, but only to persuade him that there were no such short-cuts to knowledge. Knowledge has to be obtained by studying at the feet of a guru. But Yavakri was so adamant that Indra ultimately relented and let him have his wish fulfilled.

Bharadwaja, being a man of wisdom, was anxious lest the triumph turn his son's head and cautioned Yavakri against delusions of omnipotence. And his fears unfortunately proved well-founded and justifiable. For one of the first things Yavakri did was to corner Raibhya's daughter-in-law in a lonely spot and molest her. Yavakri's misdemeanour incensed Raibhya. He invoked the *Kritya* spirit. He tore a hair from his head and made an oblation of it to the fire. From it, sprang a woman, who looked exactly like his daughter-in-law. From another hair, he similarly brought forth a *rakshasa* (demon). Then, he sent the two to kill Yavakri.

The spirit in the form of the daughter-in-law approached Yavakri seductively and stole the urn which contained the water that made him invulnerable to danger. The *rakshasa* then chased him with a trident.

Yavakri ran towards a lake in search of water, but the lake dried up. Every spot with a bit of water in it dried up at his approach. Finally, Yavakri tried to enter his father's hermitage. But a blind man of the Sudra caste, who was guarding the gate, barred Yavakri's entry. At the very moment, the *rakshasa* killed Yavakri.

When Bhardwaja learnt from the Sudra how his son had died, he was naturally distressed. Although he knew that his son was to blame for all that had happened, he cursed Raibhya that he would die at the hand of his elder son. And then shocked at his own folly in cursing a friend, he entered fire and immolated himself.

Raibhya's two sons, Paravasu and Arvasu, were conducting a fire sacrifice for the king. One night when Paravasu was visiting his home, he mistook the black deer-skin which his father was wearing for a wild animal and unintentionally killed him.

When he realized what he had done, he cremated his father and returned to the sacrificial enclosure. There he said to his brother Arvasu: "Since you are not capable of performing the sacrifice alone, go and perform the penitential rites prescribed for Brahminicide. I'll carry on with the sacrifice."

Aravasu acted at his brother's bidding. When he returned to the sacrifice-ceremony, Paravasu turned to the king and said, "This man is a Brahmin-killer. He should not be allowed to enter the sacrificial enclosures." The king promptly ordered his servants to throw Aravasu out, although the latter kept protesting loudly that he was innocent.

Aravasu retired to the jungle and prayed to the Sun God. When the gods appeared, he asked them to restore Yavakri, Bharadwaja and Raibhya back to life and make Paravasu forget his evil act. The gods granted him the boon. When Yavakri came back to life, the gods reprimanded him on his folly and asked him to pursue knowledge in the right manner.[3]

The Play's Theme and the Story

In this play, Karnad skilfully exploits the myth of Yavakri and that of Indra-Vritra to focus on the negative and positive impulses of human beings, the immoral qualities of the priestly class and how they dominate and exploit the lower class people. The play also highlights the innocent, pure and natural world of the lower castes. The love story of Arvasu and Nittilai which begins as a sub-plot grows in significance and, towards the climax, occupies the centre-stage.

The Fire and the Rain is divided into three acts along with Prologue and Epilogue. By making some alterations in the original story, Karnad unfolds the inner mind of each character. The central action of the play focuses on the motif of revenge, futility of false knowledge and the feebleness of human nature. In order to make his play more effective and relevant to the contemporary society, Karnad deviates from the original episode at several places. Besides, he has introduced a few additional characters like Nittilai, the tribals, and the actors who together with Arvasu make up the sub-plot.

Bhardwaja and Raibhya, the two friends in the myth are made as brothers in the play and their sons become cousins. Again he makes Vishakha as a lover of Yavakri. In the myth, Raibhya creates the female spirit from his hair that resembles his daughter-in-law Vishakha and asks her to assist the Brahma Rakshasa in the killing of Yavakri. However, in the play, Vishakha herself goes to Yavakri to inform him about the impending danger. Raibhya's character is also altered considerably. He is made to appear as lustful, suspicious, jealous, and a revengeful murderer. In the myth, Paravasu kills his father unintentionally but, in the play, it is done deliberately. In the myth, the Brahma Rakshasa goes to live with the female spirit, but in the play, he wants liberation from his state of limbo between life and death.

The most vital change is made in the character of Arvasu. In the play, he is not a learned priest. On the contrary, he is shown as an artist in the drama. Arvasu is seen to be in deep love with a tribal girl, Nittilai and wishes to marry her. Through the sincere and honest love of Arvasu and Nittilai, Karnad raises the problem of the caste system. Paravasu's character as the immoral Chief Priest of the fire sacrifice remains unchanged.

The structural plan of *The Fire and the Rain* runs into three parallel streams: Raibhya and Vishakha at the hermitage, the sacrificial place with Paravasu as the Chief Priest, and story of Nittilai and Arvasu with the company of the theatre.

The most significant addition to the myth in the play is the story of Indra and Vritra taken from the *Rigveda.* It is very effectively presented through the play-within-a-play enacted by the troupe of actors and Arvasu to emphasize the treachery of a brother against brother. Commenting on the inclusion of Indra-Vritra myth in the play Karnad himself aptly remarks:

> The tale of Aravasu and Paravasu fascinated me as an unusual variant of this Indian obsession with fratricide… I cannot remember when I decided to incorporate the Indra-Vritra legend in my plot, but years later, while re-reading the original version, I was astonished to find that right at the beginning of the tale of Yavakri.[4]

The play starts with the Prologue which presents the complicated details of the fire sacrifice ceremony. The entire action of the play centres on the ritual of fire sacrifice. As the play begins, it is noticed that the land is drought-ridden. So, the king of this region has made up his mind to conduct a fire sacrifice in order to propitiate Indra, the god of rains.

Paravasu, the elder son of Raibhya, is the Chief Priest who conducts the ceremony of a seven-year-long fire-sacrifice with several other priests. As the afternoon session of the fire-sacrifice is over, the Actor-Manager of a troupe comes there and requests them to grant him a permission to stage a play in honour of the fire sacrifice.

The prologue throws light on the inner world of "the characters that represents them as the embodiment of fiery desires (trishna) and, ironically, it is in the fire that they seek final liberation: Yavakri in the funeral fire and Paravasu in the sacrificial fire. We are tempted to perceive fire as a pervasive symbol in all its potentials in the play."[5]

The first act focuses on the issue of love-marriage of Nittilai, a tribal girl and Arvasu, a younger son of Raibhya. While conversing with Nittilai and Arvasu, Andhaka, in the role of *sutradhar*—actor, refers to the penance and achievements of Yavakri, the son of sage Bharadwaja. Karnad has ironically used Yavakri's penance to criticize the typical tendency of the Brahmins to attain universal knowledge for fulfilling their private ends.

Soon after his return, Yavakri learns that Vishakha, his childhood mate, has married to Paravasu, his rival cousin. He meets her in a lonely place in the forest. She succumbs to Yavakri's fascinating words after her initial resistance. Raibhya considers it an offence, an insult to the entire family. To take revenge on Yavakri, he creates "Kritya" spirit, i.e. Brahma Rakshasa. Vishakha informs Yavakri her father-in-law's evil intention. But he is quite confident of his safety, since he has the consecrated water with him to take revenge on her family. This knowledge makes Vishakha to turn the tables on Yavakri by pouring all the sanctified water from his *kamandalu*. To save his life anyhow, he starts running to reach his father's hermitage. Ironically, Andhaka stops him entering his own father's hermitage. The Brahma Rakshasa appears there and kills him with the trident.

In the second act, Paravasu, against the rules of the fire sacrifice, returns home to meet his wife. The knowledge of her wife's seduction by Yavakri as well as by his own father and his (father's) feeling of jealousy for not getting the role of the Chief Priest of the fire sacrifice renders him infuriated and outraged. Ultimately, he kills his father with his arrow in cold blood.

Paravasu goes back to complete the fire sacrifice asking Arvasu to perform the rites of penitence. But to Arvasu's surprise, Paravasu treacherously blames him of killing his father, when the former reaches the sacrificial area, after performing all the funeral rites of his father. In the assault, made by the Brahmins and the king on the order of Paravasu, Arvasu gets wounded.

What Arundhati Banerjee states about Vijay Tendulkar's play *The Vultures* fits well for Karnad's *The Fire and the Rain* also:

> The beating up of the father by his own sons,...*the mutual hatred* among the members of family underline *the fundamental evil inherent in human nature.*[6] (Italicization is the researcher's, for emphasis)

The third act starts with Nittilai, now a married woman, comes to Arvasu to nurse him back to health. The play juxtaposes the contrasting situations. The playwright, here, explores the two worlds: (i) a stormy, sentimental world that is characterized by greed, wickedness, sensuality, and (ii) a fragile, sensitive world that is characterized by love and generosity. Raibhya, Paravasu, and Yavakri represent a world of villainy, malice and ill-will, whereas Nittilai and Arvasu represent a world of love and benevolence.

The act concludes with the instruction of the Actor-Manager to Arvasu about the rules of mask performance. The Epilogue takes the audience from the world of Yavakri to that of Indra-Vishwarupa and Vritra the play-within-a-play, in which Arvasu is going to perform the role of Vritra, the demon.

Vishwarupa and Vritra, sons of Brahma, meet and embrace each other. Indra, their eldest brother feels jealous of Vishwarupa thinking that his greatness and popularity has eclipsed his personality. So, he decides to kill him. In order to succeed in his plan, Indra organizes a fire sacrifice and invites Vishwarupa. The moment Vishwarupa tries to enter along with Vritra, Indra stops him objecting to the company of Vritra being a demon, a Rakshas. When Vishwarupa was offering oblations to the gods, Indra moves behind and plunges his thunderbolt into Vishwarupa's back. Vishwarupa collapses with a loud scream.

This event of fratricide, enacted on the stage, renders Paravasu guilt-conscious. By using the Brechtian technique of theatre-audience contact, Karnad throws light on the reciprocal relationship between the theatre and life. Brahma Rakshasa who is pleading Paravasu for his release, now leaves him. The audience is greatly perplexed at the increasing sounds and gestures on the stage. Indra's vicious laughter, Vishwarupa's heart-rending screaming and Paravasu's anxious outburst—all seem mounting towards terrific emotional explosion.

Arvasu, forgetting that he is acting, is about to attack Indra (Actor-Manager). However, Nittilai comes and takes off his mask of Vritra. Her interference makes Arvasu normal. But at the same moment, her brother and husband reach the spot and she is killed mercilessly with a knife by her husband. She dies like a sacrificial animal. Arvasu takes her corpse to the sacrificial place. The voice of Indra is heard from the skies, saying, "Arvasu, son, do not grieve.... Ask for any boon and it shall be granted" (173). Arvasu wants the life of his beloved to be restored, but the Brahma Rakshasa implores him for his own release. Arvasu, remembering Nittilai's benevolent nature, asks Indra to release Brahma Rakshasa. The play ends in rains. Rain is there not because of sacrificial ritual, but because of the human sacrifice in the form of Nittilai and the grand and noble self-sacrifice of Arvasu.

Thus, the Shakespearian technique of the play-within-a-play bridges the gulf between the main plot and the sub-plot and it brings about a reversal of events.

Critical Interpretation and Appraisal of the Play

The play originally written in Kannada is titled as *Agni Mattu Male*. The playwright himself explains the broader meaning of the word 'Agni'. He writes:

> Agni is the Sanskrit word for fire and being a Sanskrit word, it carries, even when used in Kannada, connotations of holiness, of ritual status, of ceremony, which the Kannada word for fire (benki) does not possess. Agni is what burns in sacrificial altars, acts as a witness at weddings and is lit at cremations. It is also the name of the god of fire.

The fire connotes both the negative and positive human impulses such as anger, jealousy, revenge, betrayal, and lust. The rain, on the contrary, denotes the rain of human love and sacrifice, compassion, forgiveness, revival and regeneration. Commenting of various meanings of Agni, P. Jayalakshmi appropriately states: Agni works as anger and revenge in Raibhya, Paravasu, and Yavakri. In Vishakha, it burns as lust; and in the people as hunger due to the persisting drought. In all of them, except in Vishakha, Agni burns as sacrificial fire without its accompanying grace as vision or light. However, this apparently over-arching element of Agni (Fire) in the title of the play burns to convey the lessons the human being must learn about the subjugation of one's ego to the Universal Being. Much of the agony in the lives of the major characters is played out on the canvas of human consciousness till they learn this all-essential lesson of humility.[7]

The play depicts various problems such as the caste system, patriarchy, man-woman relationship, existentialism, the problem of identity, and loneliness, etc. Through the myth of Yavakri, the play explores the futility of false knowledge and evils resulting from pride, jealousy, lust, and anger. Yavakri, Raibhya and Paravasu are the victims of egoism and they misappropriate their knowledge for avenging one another. The worlds of Yavakri, Raibhya and Paravasu are characterized by hypocrisy, hatred, treachery, violence and revenge. The seduction of Vishakha by her own father-in-law and brother-in-law, the killing of the father by his own son, and that of the nephew by his uncle (indirectly), the brother's attempt to catch his own brother in his treacherous trap throw light on the fundamental evil that resides in human nature. The pursuit of knowledge does not make them free from evils resulting from pride, jealousy, lust and revenge.

Another important theme, the playwright wants to focus is the perennial problem of the caste system. The fire sacrifice is organized to propitiate the god of rains. Low caste people are prohibited to enter the holy area. Priests are directed not to leave the precincts and not talk to the *shudras* and not to give themselves to sensual pleasures.

The play is Karnad's comment on caste as well as gender-biased society. Both the female characters try their best to raise a voice of rebellion. But the extent of their resistance is determined by the gender and caste group to which they belong. It is also observed that their characters are shaped by their respective social positions. Jayalakshmi is quite justified in pointing out:

> "He (Karnad) re-interprets and re-presents the myth to make a definitive statement in the context of the present.

> He re-constitutes the ancient myth with fresh revisionary meaning with the additional dimension of gender and caste by creating the narrative of Arvasu and Nittilai. Nittilai is as oppressed as Vishakha or may be even more, but the oppression in the latter is unnecessary and avoidable. As a member of a family of the learned men trained in leading disciplined life, such treatment for Vishakha is unjustified. In the case of Nittilai, the suffering is due to the caste division and gender bias in society and ignorance of men in her community: thus, suffering is made unavoidable and inescapable.[8]

To quote Jayalakshmi, again,

> Nittilai and Vishakha are both victims of male control, consequent to which is the oppression and exploitation inflicted upon them by the often violent heterogeneous male subjects. Nittilai seems to suffer double marginalization, as is often the lot of communities divided on the lines of caste and colour: she is marginalized from the mainstream as belonging to Sudra caste. In her own community, she is presented as one demanding her right to take a life partner of her choice.[9]

Nittilai and Vishakha appear to be in the search for identity. Both of them suffer from the problem of anonymity. Although Vishakha belongs to an upper-caste Brahmin family, her position is not far different from that of Nittilai. Her social position does not provide her with any privilege. Throughout her life, she is dominated by her so-called learned male counterparts. Nittilai belongs to the family of hunters. Both of them are the victims of the male-dominated society in which they are subjected equally to violent displacement and silencing. These women characters bring to notice the stark reality of the society that women have been used by their male counterparts as stepping stones in their power-struggle. No doubt, they try to challenge that oppression but, in the process, they meet with a tragic end. Suffering is their lot, a badge of their tribe. It is so, because

> ...humanity is male and man defines woman not in herself but as relative to him,...she is the incidental,

> the inessential as opposed to the essential. He is...the Absolute; she is the Other.[10]

Both the women characters appear to be the witnesses of womankind's endless suffering in the male-dominated society. That is why Jayalakshmi is quite justified in pointing out: "Vishakha and Nittilai, thus, are not mere literary constructs but women real and material, carrying within them their collective histories as women.... The need is for a sympathetic understanding of their oppressive past in grappling with our present-day reality in which also lies real humanity."[11]

Thus, the position of women in the patriarchal system of society is one of the major thematic concerns of Karnad's plays. The women characters in the play are necessarily and inevitably, the victims of patriarchy. Vishakha is exploited by her husband, father-in-law and her former lover. She becomes a sexual instrument in the hands of the male characters to avenge each other. Similarly, Nittilai also becomes a victim of the tribal patriarchy. Mala Ranganathan's observation with regard to the oppression of Vishakha and Nittilai in the patriarchal culture is worth considering; she remarks: "The brahminical patriarchy in the play reduces the woman to sexual exploitation and neglect by men vying with one another for knowledge and power. Simple as it may appear to be, the tribal patriarchy also proves to be lethal towards women who do not abide by the community rules framed by the male elders."[12]

Vishakha's loneliness in the male-centric world is very effectively presented in the play. She suffers from loneliness because of her selfish and treacherous lover and her self-centred husband. P. Jayalakshmi aptly describes the miserable state of Vishakha by comparing her lonely life to the image of an empty water-pot. She comments, "The image of an empty water-pot covered with cobwebs, lying in a corner, discarded, to be replenished with life-giving water, is suggestive metaphorically of the condition of Vishakha's life—dry, barren and empty."[13]

Existentialism seems to be one of the dominant motifs in the Karnad play and *The Fire and the Rain* is no exception to it. The characters here are found in the grip of the existential dilemma. It is because of his strong hatred for Paravasu, Yavakri is unable to understand the meaning of knowledge. He projects the image of an existential character and shows that a few men are able to make a correct choice. Arvasu also finds himself in existential situation when he is terribly shocked at the treachery of his brother, Paravasu. There are several instances in the play which throw light on how the principal characters confront the existential problems. Thus, the play, in general, treats of such existential themes as unfulfilment of love, the illusion of friendship and brotherhood, the isolation and alienation of man, the lack of communication and the quest for identity and meaning in an uncertain and often incomprehensible world, etc.

Conclusion

In *The Fire and the Rain,* Karnad has succeeded in projecting harsh realities of the modern civilization, which is characterized by stress, strain, confusion, frustration, loneliness, disintegration, and meaninglessness. While depicting the vices and drawbacks of both an individual and society, Karnad's humanitarian approach and his commitment to human values become clearly perceptible. Although the theme of revenge, hatred, violence pervades the entire atmosphere, the play marks the triumph of truth over untruth, of goodness over evil. That is why the play ends in rains that symbolize a life-giving force. To conclude the discussion in the words of Jayalakshmi, "Here the famine is real and metaphorical. The intent of traditional Yoga 'marga' is not self-mortification, nor the end of all sacrifice for personal gain, but to make the body a perfect instrument of the spirit. That ultimate knowledge Nittilai gains and Arvasu learns, staying in the midst of life, not away from or outside it—a sign of true perfection."[14]

Notes

1. Bhaskar Chandavarkar, Quoted in Aparna Dharwadker Bhargava. "Introduction". Girish Karnad. *Collected Plays.* Volume 2. New Delhi: OUP, 2005, xvi.
2. Aparna Bhargava Dharwadker, "Introduction". *op. cit.*, xvi-xvii.
3. Girish Karnad, *Appendix*-1 "Note on *The Fire and the Rain.*" *Collected Plays. op. cit.*, 291-93.
4. *Ibid.*, 296-97.

5. Vanashree Tripathi, "*The Fire and the Rain*: A Tragedy of Desires". *Three Plays of Girish Karnad: A Study in Poetics and Culture*. New Delhi: Prestige, 2004, 139.
6. Arundhati Banerjee, "Introduction". *Five Plays of Vijay Tendulkar*. Bombay: OUP, 1992, xii.
7. P. Jayalakshmi, "Politics of Power: A Study of Gender and Caste in *The Fire and the Rain*". *Girish Karnad's Plays: Performance and Critical Perspectives*. Ed. Tutun Mukherjee. Delhi: Pencraft International, 2006, 253.
8. *Ibid.*, 261.
9. *Ibid.*, 255.
10. Simone de Beauvoir, "Introduction". *The Second Sex*. New York: Vintage, 1989, xxii.
11. P. Jayalakshmi, *op. cit.*, 262.
12. Mala Ranganathan, "Re-Reading *The Fire and the Rain*". *Girish Karnad's Plays. op. cit.*, 267.
13. P. Jayalakshmi, *op. cit.*, 261.
14. *Ibid.*, 262-63.

HISTORY PLAYS

5

Tughlaq: From Idealism to Realism

Introduction

Tughlaq (1964), Karnad's second play, is the most popular and the most forceful play. It marks the beginning of the 'New Drama' in India. Eunice de Souza criticizes Indian drama in English saying, "Indian plays in English do not go back to history to establish modern man's relationship to history, to interpret contemporary problems, to work out ideas through historical material and do not establish the modern Indian relation to history."[1] Tughlaq is a fitting rejoinder to this criticism. It has been a grand success both in print and on the stage. The merits of this play are manifest in the eponymous character of Muhammad bin Tughlaq and its contemporaneity. In the "Introduction" to the English version of the play, Karnad has stated that it reflected the mood of political disillusionment the country faced after the Nehru era of idealism.[2] Historically, it was the story of the most intelligent and visionary Sultan of Delhi, who in his attempts to fulfil his ideals, perpetuated their opposites.

Tughlaq was first written and staged in Kannada and later rendered into English by the author himself in 1971. Muhammad bin Tughlaq of Delhi, a Muslim Sultan of the 14th century, has been a colourful personality. His rule seems to be the combination of paradoxes related to idealism, foresightedness, great administrative reforms and violence, ruthlessness, bloodshed and barbarity. It is a historical play concerned with the life and tumultuous reign of Muhammad bin Tughlaq for about twenty-six years. For the artistic purpose and compactness of dramatic structure, Karnad has selected only five years from 1327 to

1332. The action of the play takes place in Delhi in the year 1327, then on the road from Delhi to Daulatabad, and lastly in and around the fort in Daulatabad five years later. For presenting the complexity of Tughlaq's character, the playwright chiefly relies on the contemporary historians like Zia-ud-Din Barani's *Tarikh-i-Firoz Shahi* (1351), Al-Marshi's *The Maslik-al-absar*, Ibn-i-Battuta's *Travels* and Badoni's *Tarikh-i-Mubarak Shahi*. And particularly "Using Barani's basic narrative, his attitudes, and portions of his text, Karnad arranges the thirteen scenes of *Tughlaq* as a sequence of self-cancelling actions that articulate both political and psychological ironies."[3] This play explores the paradoxical nature of Tughlaq whose reign is known as one of the spectacular regimes of history.

Albert Camus' *Caligula* is considered to be the source of inspiration for *Tughlaq* which provided both the absurd conception of the human situation and the technique of handling a historical myth for the modern theatre. The play is described as a historical play, because the principal character of the play who plays the protagonist's role is taken from history and the events that constitute the framework for the plot of the play are documented as historical events. Veena Noble Dass points out, "*Tughlaq* is much more than a chronicle play, because rather than the mere sequential presentation of facts and events taken from recorded history, it reconstructs very imaginatively some of the most significant events in the life of a remarkable king, not only in relation to a particular period in India's national history but in terms of India's contemporary times. It is in fact a detached and objective study of an important era with Muhammad bin Tughlaq at the centre—a dramatic interpretation of the process of history in terms of individual character, of how history is made (or unmade?) by a great monarch who is extraordinary intelligent, far-seeing, and idealistic but unpredictable, impulsive and whimsical."[4]

In *Tughlaq*, Karnad explores the paradox of Muhammad bin Tughlaq, the idealistic Sultan of Delhi whose reign is considered to be one of the most spectacular failures in Indian history. In his interview by Rajinder Paul, Girish Karnad explains:

> What struck me absolutely about Tughlaq's history was that it was contemporary. The fact that here was the most idealistic, the most intelligent king ever to come on the throne of Delhi—and one of the greatest failures also. And within a span of twenty years this tremendously capable man had gone to pieces. This seemed to be both due to his idealism as well as the shortcomings within him, such as his impatience, his cruelty, his feeling that he had the only correct answer.[5]

The Play's Theme and Story

Karnad tries to maintain fidelity to the historical sources which present Tughlaq as a combination of opposites—a dreamer and a man of action, benevolent and cruel, theistic and atheistic. Both in history and in the play, Tughlaq is a great learned person—an idealist and a visionary. While maintaining the historical facts, Karnad artistically reconstructs some of the significant events that took place in the Sultan's life. And thus, he deftly exploits history for raising social, religious and political issues of the age which seem to have direct bearing on the present socio-political and religious situations.

Karnad projects Tughlaq in various roles. Tughlaq stands for administrative reforms, for Hindu-Muslim amity, recognition of merit, despite caste and creed, restructuring of administrative machinery and reformation of taxation, establishment of a well-balanced society in which all shall enjoy freedom, justice, equality and basic human rights. As a man of letters, he tries to implement a new system in his administration. Being a rationalist and a philosopher, he completely deviates from the religious doctrines in respect of politics and administration. Therefore, the orthodox Muslim leaders show their vigorous protest against the Sultan for his departure from the holy tenets of religion. They consider him a non-believer in Islam as he cancels the jiziya tax. Tughlaq's tolerance for the Hindus is bitterly criticized. At the very beginning of the play, in scene one, the conversation between an old man and a young man reveals the tension and dramatic conflict between the two factions—the followers and the opponents of Tughlaq:

Old Man: God, what's this country coming to!

Young Man: What are you worried about, grandfather? The country's in perfectly safe hands—safer than any you've seen before. (147)

Here, the old man represents orthodox Muslims and the Young Man represents the liberal viewpoint of the Sultan. It is very clear that at the very beginning of the play the conflict is set in between the old and the new, orthodox religion and modernity. And as the plot advances, the conflict also mounts up. The orthodox people think that the country is not in safe hands, because Tughlaq is liberal to the Hindus. The abolition of jiziya tax on the Hindus infuriates them. They do not understand Tughlaq's idealism and reformatory zeal. Therefore, they condemn him as an enemy of Islam. However, the young people admire and support the secular and liberal policies of the Sultan. As a matter of fact, Tughlaq seems to be a devout Muslim with strong faith in the holy *Koran* but his rationalistic and ideal views are beyond the understanding of the orthodox people. He wants to build such a society where people of different communities live in harmony.

Tughlaq calls upon his countrymen to extend him their support and co-operation for implementing his plans. Thus, the first scene presents him as an idealistic performer who hopes to lead his people into a Utopia. But unfortunately his generous intention is misunderstood by the orthodox Muslims. They think that he is betraying Islam by flouting its ideals and practices. The Hindus are also suspicious of the Sultan's good intention. So, it is observed that "in an age of religious fanaticism and hostility between Hindus and Muslims, his (Tughlaq's) broad-minded religious tolerance seems foolish to the Muslims and cunning to the Hindus who suspect his motives".[6]

The Sultan introduces several reformative measures for the benefit of his subjects. "But the only character to benefit from this utopian move is a low-caste Muslim washer-man, Aziz, who assumes the identity of a poor Hindu Brahmin to win a false judgment against the Sultan and secure a position at the court."[7] However, the Sultan is not aware of the fact that the opportunists like Aziz in the disguise of Vishnu Prasad misappropriate reformative activities which therefore fail to reach the people whom they are meant for. In the opening scene, we find one more announcement of the Sultan. He declares his crucial decision of shifting the capital of his empire from Delhi to Daulatabad. At this, his people are greatly shocked and they react in bewilderment. The Sultan clarifies his intention of changing the capital by stating:

> My empire is large now and embraces the south and I need a capital which is at its heart. Delhi is too near the border and as you well know its peace is never free from the fear of invaders. But for me the most important factor is that Daulatabad is a city of the Hindus and as the capital it will symbolize the bond between Muslims and Hindus which I wish to develop and strengthen in my Kingdom. (149)

The Sultan takes this decision to create an effective administrative centre in Deccan. But his hasty decision generates great discontent against him. It causes unimaginable and untold suffering to the people. The Sultan is accused of killing his father and brother at prayer time and is considered to be guilty of patricide and fratricide.

The final scene depicts the disastrous end of Tughlaq's reign. It is informed that Tughlaq is greatly shocked to know of the murder of Aazam at the mouth of the secret tunnel from the palace. The famine riots have already spread. Daulatabad appears to be a devastated place full of massacre and bloodshed. Even Barani wants to leave the place. Aziz, in the disguise of Ghiyas-ud-din, goes to the palace to bless the Sultan and the people and to purify Daulatabad. Thus, it is only in the last scene that the Sultan sees a parody of himself and his whole career in his unmasking by the scoundrel and cheat, the washerman Aziz. This scene reveals the greatest irony of fate and also of situation in which the Sultan realizes the futility of his utopia. Completely broken in mind and body, he once again proclaims his decision to move the capital back to Delhi. Finally, he gives himself to sleep which has eluded him for all these years.

Critical Interpretation and Appraisal of the Play

Although the play is based on one of the historical incidents, it has a contemporary relevance. Karnad himself finds a parallel between Muhammad and Nehru: "And I felt, in the early sixties, India had also come very far in the same direction—the twenty-year period seemed to me very much a striking parallel."[8] However, there is something more than this parallelism. While commenting on the idealism of Muhammad, Aparna Dharwadker states: "The first is the untenability of the idealistic and visionary politics that Nehru and Mahatma Gandhi practiced as national leaders and valorized in their respective meditations on political action—*The Discovery of India* and *The Story of My Experiments with Truth*."[9] She thinks the second phase of Sultan's reign resembles the rule of Mrs. Indira Gandhi.

Muhammad feels that he is far superior to any other in his enlightenment and idealism. He does not accept any alternative to his idealistic decisions and, therefore, tries to do what he thinks is good for his people without their nodding. The play not only depicts Tughlaq as a great failure both as a man and as an administrator. It also shows his madness that could have been the reason behind the radical changes he has tried to initiate in his kingdom.

With his aim of bringing reformation in his kingdom, he changes the tax-system and shifts his capital from Delhi to Devgiri, later renamed as Daulatabad. The other reform he introduces is the radical re-organization of the coinage system and to re-determine the relative value of precious metals. Similarly, he starts the system of token currency with the use of copper coins. However, the idea has not been analyzed and/or examined with its props and cons before its implementation. It leads to its misuse and ultimately, results in corruption. He makes the prayer compulsory throughout the kingdom. Doing so, he has invited trouble instead of winning the appreciation and admiration of the Muslims. All his brilliant ideas are doomed to fail since they have been implemented impulsively. None of his schemes, however, well-intentioned, is understood or appreciated by his people and none of them proves successful.

The people misuse his ideas for personal gains. Impracticability, thus, turns out to be sole root-cause of his grievous failure.

Karnad portrays Tughlaq as a man having a dual personality: he is a clever, ruthless administrator and a sensitive poet-philosopher. He is not able to restore balance, within himself, between his dreams and his practical duties as a ruler, though he declares that it is his ardent, heartfelt desire to bring about a transformation in all walks of life. Most of the problems, encountered by Tughlaq, are the result of his inability to reconcile the polarities of his own nature and of the tensions between dream and reality.

"Had the population of his kingdom been of a homogeneous culture, perhaps Tughlaq would not have faced as many difficulties as he did. The schism in his nature is aggravated by the schism that divided his people."[10] When the emperor continues to maintain an image of impartiality, the Muslims plan to exploit the opportunity and trap him in his own virtue. The Sultan shifts the capital to Daulatabad from Delhi with the desire to balance the power of the Delhi-based Muslims with that of the Daulatabad-based Hindus. The Muslims of Delhi are strongly opposed to this decision. Similarly, his plan "to introduce copper currency and bring it on a par with silver coins would appear to suggest economic astuteness but he lacks the foresight to see the possibility of misuse of the whole experiment. The clever swindlers Aziz and Azam exploit the situation and are able to sabotage the entire economic system of the kingdom."[11]

Muhammad has a dual aim behind all his actions: (1) to create an ideal society and (2) to acquire name, fame, and a public image of impartiality. However, the clever, shrewd king cannot reconcile himself to dreamer and the poet-philosopher in him. These two contradictory aspects of his nature remain polarized and invite troubles and result in failure of his plans. Events go beyond his control and consequently, he finds himself unable to prevent his ruin. His dispassionate idealism is, thus, defeated by the stark reality of his deeds and misdeeds.

Conclusion

The play is Karnad's comment on the contemporary situation in the post-colonial Indian society. While focusing on the contemporaneity of the play, he also stresses the fact that it is not a political allegory. In his interview by Paul, he remarks that the twenty-year period of Tughlaq's decline offered a 'striking parallel' to the first two decades of Indian independence under Nehru's idealistic but troubled leadership and that Nehru resembled Tughlaq in his propensity for failure despite an extraordinary intellectual calibre. Yet the play was not meant to be either an "obvious comment on Nehru" or an "exact parallel" of the past and the present. In a 1989 essay on the Indian theatre, Karnad observes, again, in the context of *Tughlaq*, that the most interesting feature of the politics of the 1960 was "the way the newly enfranchised electorate was slowly becoming aware of the power placed in its hands for the first time in history. The other equally visible movement was the gradual displacement of pre-independence idealism by hard-nosed political cynicism" (Theatre 342). The nation's disenchantment with visionary leadership and the consequent emergence of a populist politics, thus, appear to be, for Karnad, the most compelling contemporary referents for his historical drama with its allowing fictionality.[12]

In Tughlaq's dream, one can see Mahatma Gandhi's idealism. In his weapon of satyagraha, he expects a state of complete preparedness in the leader as well as in his followers. At the beginning of the play, Tughlaq also appears to possess such a state. He wants his people to follow him, but only if they have complete faith in him. At this stage, he seems to be a "religious actualist" whose "very passion and power make him want to make actual for others what actualizes him".[13]

The analogies with Mahatma Gandhi and Nehru thus foreground the more or less well-intentioned idealism of Tughlaq-Barani in the first half and suppress the cruelty, repressiveness, and cunning of Tughlaq-Aziz in the second. The analogies with Indira Gandhi reverse this emphasis and bring the two halves of the play together. For Romesh Thapar, the contradictory traits in Tughlaq's personality find echo in Indira Gandhi's personality. In the political mythology of the nation, Indira Gandhi appears as both demon and goddess, emasculating widow and nurturing mother (Gupte 18-22); in journalistic and scholarly writing she is a "mixture of paradoxes", a sign of the "amoral politics" of the late 1960s, and a pragmatist "political to the very soul" (Malik and Vajpeyi 13, 22). But she is closest to Karnad's protagonist in her propensity for choosing evil out of a compulsion to act for the nation and in the self-destructive role/nature of her authoritarianism.[14]

The play *Tughlaq* is a classic as it crosses the boundaries of temporality and historicity. The situations depicted and the characters portrayed belong to all times and climes. The fictional Tughlaq evokes Jawaharlal Nehru, Mahatma Gandhi, and Indira Gandhi, but he goes beyond this. Sometimes, he evokes only himself. Aparna Dharwadker is quite right in pointing out: "A historical poem or play is textually complex and culturally vital, precisely because its narrative originates in other (often problematic) narratives and possesses meaning independent of specific topical contexts.[15]

Notes

1. Eunice de Souza, "Some Recent Indian Plays in English". *Perspectives on Indian Drama in English*. Eds. M.K. Naik and S. Mokashi Punekar. Madras: OUP, 1977, 160.
2. Girish Karnad, "Interview". *Tughlaq*. *Enact*. June, 1971.
3. Aparna Dharwadker, "Historical Fictions and Postcolonial Representation: Reading *Tughlaq*". *Karnad's Plays: Performance and Critical Perspectives*. Ed. Tutun Mukherjee. New Delhi: Pencraft International, 2006, 98.
4. Veena Noble Dass, "Use and Abuse of History in *Tughlaq*." *Girish Karnad's Plays: Performance and Critical Perspectives. op. cit.*, 91.
5. Rajinder Paul, "Girish Karnad Interviewed". *Enact*. June, 1971, 54.
6. Christine Gomez, "Karnad's *Tughlaq* as an Alienated Protagonist". *The Plays of Girish Karnad: Critical Perspectives*. Ed. J. Dodiya. New Delhi: Prestige, 1999, 114.
7. Aparna Dharwadker, *op. cit.*, 98.

8. Girish Karnad, "Interview". *op. cit.*
9. Aparna Dharwadker, *op. cit.*, 103.
10. Basavaraj S. Naikar, "*Tughlaq* as an Experimenter". *Girish Karnad's Plays: Performance and Critical Perspectives. op. cit.*, 88.
11. *Ibid.*, 89.
12. Aparna Dharwadker, *op. cit.*, 107.
13. *Ibid.*, 109.
14. *Ibid.*, 111-12.
15. *Ibid.*, 117.

6

Tale-Danda: Karnadian Utopia

Introduction

> Where the world has not been broken up into fragments, into narrow domestic walls.... Into that heaven of freedom, my father, let my country awake.[1]

says Rabindranath Tagore in one of his songs from *Gitanjali*. However, this idealism is not transformed into realism. Ultimately, the heaven of freedom, Tagore speaks of, has remained a dream forever. W.B. Yeats in his revolutionary, epoch-making poem, reveals the universal truth:

> The best lack all conviction, while the worst
> Are full of passionate intensity.[2]

The incidents that manifest hatred between man and man and result in merciless violence were not unexpected occurrences in the post-Gandhian society. Thus, the freedom-fighters' dream of demolishing the stratification of Hindu society on caste grounds was repeatedly shattered.[3]

Karnad's play *Tale-Danda* best illustrates the shattering of the dream of a casteless, egalitarian society. The play depicts the story of the community that existed in the twelfth century kingdom in Karnataka ruled by the King Bijjala. The incident, narrated in the story, took place in 1168 A.D. At the centre of the play is Basavanna, a saintly person, a pioneer of the Bhakti Movement in Karnataka. Basavanna, who dreams of a casteless society, is a spiritual leader who wants to bring about a change in the mind-set of the people. He works as a royal treasurer. Fascinated and thrilled by his egalitarian and secular thinking, thousands of common people become his disciples who come to be recognized as the *sharanas*. These devotees come largely from the economically oppressed lower castes/classes.

The play comprises three acts. The scenes I to IV are incorporated in act one, scenes V and VI are included in act two, and act three consists of scenes VII to XVI. The first act revolves round the central character Basavanna, his confrontation with Prince Sovideva for being accused of theft and its ultimate results. The second act explores in detail the repercussions resulting out of the marital proposal of a Brahmin girl, Kalavati the daughter of Madhuvarsa with a cobbler's boy Sheelavanta, the son of Haralaya. The play reaches its climax in the third act that delineates King Bijjala's imprisonment by his own son, Jagdeva's rebellion in which he kills the king, and commits suicide. While portraying the characters, Karnad remains a detached observer, neither moralizing nor philosophizing in any way. He represents them as they are—realistically, and not idealistically. Although the play is full of action mostly bloody and violent, the tender aspect of human relationship are noticeable. Basavanna meets a mysterious death in the end. So, his sincere attempt at creating a casteless society ends in frustration.

While Basavanna's appeal and secular teaching encourage more and more people to embrace the faith of the *sharanas*, there grows an increasing fear among the members of the upper castes of being overwhelmed[4] by their adversaries.

The movement initiated by the *sharanas* for the establishment of social justice, freedom, and equality challenges the cultural practices that place the upper caste people in a privileged position. The intercaste marriage of the Brahmin girl with a cobbler boy enhances the confidence of the *sharanas*. However, this daring act results into the revolt of the *sharanas* against the establishment. The movement leads to the reign of terror and results into massacre and bloodshed.

The Play's Theme and Story

Bijjala, a barber becomes the king of Kalyan. He is well aware of his roots. So, he says, "For ten generations my forefathers ravaged the land as robber barons. For another five, they ruled as the trusted feudatories of the emperor himself.

They married into every royal family in sight. Bribed generations of Brahmins with millions of cows. All this so they could have the caste of Kshatriya branded on their foreheads" (14). Bijjala also marries a royal princess Rambhavati and has a son by her named Sovideva.

Bijjala thinks that his city flourishes because of *sharanas*' hard work and devotion, and therefore, feels grateful to them and their leader Basavanna. Unlike his father, Sovideva hates the *sharanas* and Basavanna. He grows suspicious that Basavanna spends a large amount of money from the royal treasury on his hospitality to his guests. He wants to prove this by inspecting the treasury so that he can win his father's favour.

Sovideva's attempt ends in failure. Jagdeva, a *sharana*, gathers thousands of *sharanas* to protect the royal treasury in Basavanna's absence and prevents Sovideva from tampering with it. He performs the task in all devotion despite the fact that his father is on the death-bed. So, after verification, the treasury is found intact. Bijjala scolds Sovideva very severely for his misbehaviour. Feeling insulted, Sovideva decides to rebel against his father and Basavanna. He is helped by Damodar Bhatta, the Queen's priest, and Manchanna Kramita, the Brahmin advisor to the king.

The death of his father makes Jagdeva remorseful and restless. He lays all the blame on Basavanna's shoulders for the loss of his father. He thinks that he protects the royal treasury disregarding his father's adverse health and the entire credit goes to Basavanna as people consider it a miracle. In a fit of anger, he supports the violence of *sharanas* against Jains at Maddur which is totally contradictory to Basavanna's principle of non-violence.

The second act starts with the *sharanas* assembled at Basavanna's house. They propose the marriage between Kalavati, a Brahmin girl and Sheelavanta, a Dalit boy. Their parents invite Basavanna to the betrothal. Thinking about the future prospects of this intercaste marriage, Basavanna gets disturbed and cannot say anything in a confused state of his mind. The *sharanas* get perturbed at his hesitation. Basavanna tries to justify his stand by saying: "It's a question of life and death for these children.

From tomorrow the wrath of the bigoted will pursue them like a swarm of snakes to strike as they pause to put up a roof or light on oven. Who will protect them then?" (45-46). The *sharanas* are so overwhelmed that they remain stubbornly stuck to their stand.

Bijjala is also against this intercaste marriage, since he fears that this marriage may lead to communal violence. He requests Basavanna to somehow stop it. However, Basavanna, too, is helpless to prevent it. Willy nilly, he comes forth to support the *sharanas*. Reluctantly, Bijjala uses his army to avert the blood bath during the marriage. Thus, the marriage takes place without any hindrance. While the *sharanas* are overjoyed considering it a great achievement, the marriage infuriates the orthodox Hindus. For them, this marriage is a great sacrilege, a violation of *shastras*' injunctions. Damodar Bhatta complains against it saying: "Indrani, the Rig Veda tells us that the four *varnas* flowed out of the Primordial Man: the Brahmin from the head, the Shudra from the feet. So, what we have here in this wedding is desecration of the body of the Purusha. How horrifying!" (62).

The third act deals with the massacre of the *sharanas* by Sovideva, who follows the advice of Damodar and Manchana. In Basavanna's absence, the *sharanas* cannot gather up their courage and go helter-skelter. He occupies the throne by imprisoning his father. The inhuman treatment given to the *sharanas* and their massacre infuriate Jagdeva. He enters the royal palace to avenge Sovideva. However, Sovideva goes to his father-in-law for safety. Frustrated Jagdeva sends his followers to the inner shrine of Shiva, where Bijjala hides himself. In keeping with Basavanna's advice, the old, helpless king embraces the Linga to protect himself. When he is told a lie that Basavanna has sent them to him, he comes out of the shrine. Violating Basavanna's preaching of non-violence, Jagdeva stabs him to death. Later on, he too commits suicide. Basavanna is greatly grieved when he comes to know of the merciless killing of the king by Jagdeva. He considers it to be the defeat of his principles. In the end, he too, meets his death mysteriously. "History comes to full circle by the end of the play with the dramatic reporting on the stage of Basavanna's death—and with him dies his vision of a casteless society."[5] The play ends with Sovideva's coronation amongst the heart-breaking cries of pains and groans. The screams of the victims and the vedic chanting are heard simultaneously.

Critical Interpretation and Appraisal of the Play

> For orthodox, it (caste) is like a skin that cannot be cast off; for the *sharanas*, it is a cast of mind that can be separated from the corporeal body and naturalized through reason. Karnad's pessimistic conclusion, which applies to the twelfth century history of the *sharanas* as well as to present-day cultural politics in India, is that caste is ultimately untranslatable, even for those who repudiate it.[6]

This is the message conveyed by Girish Karnad in *Tale-Danda*. Using history, Karnad once again, provides commentary on the power politics of the day. "In the short Preface to the English translation of *Tale-Danda* (1993), Karnad commented that he wrote the play in 1989 when the 'Mandir' and 'Mandal' movements were beginning to show again how relevant the questions posed by these thinkers (the *Virasaivas*) were for our age."[7] On the public reading of the play by the dramatist at the Natya Shodh Sanstha, he was asked the question: "Had any contemporary political event prompted the playwright to choose a theme that focused on the caste problem?" Pat came the reply from Karnad: "Why any political event? Every...each of them."[8]

Tale-Danda occupies an important place in the Karnad canon. In this play, Karnad deals with such issues as reflect the way of life and the thinking of an entire community. The play is universal since, "The events within the play offer a covert commentary on both facets of the present crisis, because Karnad seeks to enforce the identity between communal and caste violence, and to show that the effects of intra-religious conflict are very similar to those of inter-religious conflict."[9]

In *Tale-Danda*, Karnad highlights the most delicate and crucial problem of caste system that has remained burning through the different phases of the Indian history. The main reason for the defeat of Basavanna is the lack of unity and faith. The society is divided on the basis of caste, class, colour, religion, gender, etc. and these divisions are again sub-divided. That is why Kalyani and Haralayya point out: "Lalitakka, we are cobblers. Not skinners or tanners. The holeyas skin the carcass. The madigas and the dohas tan the hide. Only then does it come to us" (48). Basavanna is cheated not by his opponents but by his own followers. So, Karnad himself states, not without any justification: "Ultimately, the final betrayal was not by the enemies, but by the followers."[10]

Basavanna had a dream of an egalitarian society based on the foundation of liberty, equality, fraternity, and social justice. The movement was strongly opposed by the establishment, i.e. by the orthodox Hindus with the fear that their hold on the low-caste people would come to an end with the success of this reformist movement. Similarly, Basavanna's followers failed to understand the real aims and objectives of this movement and Basavanna's progressive ideology. In the flush of enthusiasm, they resorted to the violent means. And without being united by creed or conviction, they attempted to attain equality. For them, the intercaste marriage of a Brahmin girl with a cobbler boy is a wonderful means of achieving their goal. The ultimate result is: Basavanna's efforts to bring about a change in the mind-set of the people and thereby a complete transformation in the conventional social set-up receives a setback.

Conclusion

To sum up, the socio-political events in the current situation have prompted Karnad to write this play. It is not difficult to find the echoes of the contemporary politics of V.P. Singh's Government in the royalist regime of Kalyan. For Aparna Dharwadker rightly points out:

> Throughout *Tale-Danda* we could substitute the category of religion for the category of caste, and the terms Hindu and Muslim for the terms 'Brahmin' and 'untouchable' without modifying the play's thematic or its interlocked movements of transgression and punishment. With caste and communalism persisting as

> the dominant sources of present-day political violence in India, the relevance of *Tale-Danda* like that of *Tughlaq* appears over-determined and inexhaustible, and both the plays have taken on cautionary and prophetic qualities of similar kind.[11]

Tale-Danda, thus, exposes the ugly deformity of the Hindu society which has not undergone any great changes for ages. Basavanna has failed in his attempt at creating a casteless society. He is defeated by his own followers. The merciless killing of the helpless king by the *sharanas* makes him realize the hollowness of his idealism. "Basavanna realizes that the movement that he nurtured has gone berserk. He dies, a broken-hearted man. The *sharanas* are ruthlessly crushed and Sovideva rules in a land where the caste-system remains its sway and things become as they were before...."[12] So, Karnad makes a point in his remark: "It seems 800 years have solved no problems. We are back exactly where we started."[13] And, repeating itself, the cycle of history is complete.

The play dwells more on the construction of the plot than on the delineation of the characters. "Except for the king Bijjala, there are gaps in the development of each character."[14] Therefore, the characters, allegorical as they are, appear to be pawns in the game of chess. H.S. Krishnamurthy points out: "Bijjala stands in contrast to Basavanna. He understands the economic repercussions of the *sharanas* movement. For Bijjala, the intercaste marriage figures not just as a violation of the moral or social codes, it bears inevitable impact upon the social and political aspects of his kingdom. Karnad envisages these characters—Basavanna and Bijjala—with their dialectics in theatrical terms."[15]

Karnad has recorded the political happenings of the contemporary society in terms of allegorical events and characters. In the words of Arundhati Banerjee: "Much of the action takes place in the royal palace, at Basavanna's residence and near Jagdeva's ancestral house. The huge canvas that the play covers poses a challenge for any prospective director. *Tale-Danda*...has a big cast yet has already been successfully performed in different language versions. Karnad's only regret is that, because of immense investment in the play's language, *Tale-Danda* has lost much of its force in translation. The original Kannada version uses various dialects and vernacular inflections to represent the members of the different castes."[16]

Notes

1. Rabindranath Tagore, "Where the Mind is without Fear". *Gitanjali.* New Delhi: Macmillan, 2004, 33.
2. W.B. Yeats, "The Second Coming". *Six English Poets.* Ed. V. Sachchidanandan. New Delhi: Macmillan, 1978, 253.
3. H.S. Krishnamurthy, "*Tale-Danda*: Text and Performance". *Girish Karnad's Plays: Performance and Critical Perspectives.* Ed. Tutun Mukherjee. New Delhi: Pencraft International, 2006, 231.
4. Arundhati Banerjee, "Caste Consciousness and Karnad: Analyzing *Tale-Danda*". *Girish Karnad's Plays: Performance and Critical Perspectives. op. cit.*, 228.
5. Vanashree Tripathi, "*Tale-Danda*: Evils of Varnashrama". *Three Plays of Girish Karnad.* New Delhi. Prestige, 2004, 101.
6. Aparna Dharwadker, "Introduction". *Collected Plays: Girish Karnad.* Vol. Two. New Delhi: OUP, 2005, xii.
7. *Ibid.*
8. Arundhati Banerjee, *op. cit.*, 227.
9. Aparna Dharwadker, *op. cit.*, xiii.
10. Manchi Sarat Babu, "Social Deformity in *Tale-Danda*". *The Plays of Girish Karnad: Critical Perspectives.* Ed. J.K. Dodiya. New Delhi: Prestige, 1999, 286.
11. Aparna Dharwadker, *op. cit.*, xiii.
12. Arundhati Banerjee, *op. cit.*, 229.
13. Quoted in Manchi Sarat Babu, "Social Deformity". *Indian Drama Today: Study in the Theme of Cultural Deformity.* New Delhi: Prestige, 1997, 50.
14. Arundhati Banerjee, *op. cit.*, 230.
15. H.S. Krishnamurthy, *op. cit.*, 233.
16. Arundhati Banerjee, *op. cit.*, 229.

7

The Dreams of Tipu Sultan: Towards Nationalism

Introduction

Like his earlier plays *Tughlaq* (1964) and *Tale-Danda* (1990), this play is also a historical play which vividly depicts different facets of Tipu's personality and his great concern for India as a nation. *The Dreams of Tipu Sultan* was written for BBC's Radio to commemorate fifty years of India's Independence. It is the play which Karnad originally wrote in English and then translated into Kannada. About the creation of the play, Karnad himself says, "In 1996, the BBC commissioned me to write a radio play to celebrate the Fiftieth Anniversary of Indian Independence. The plot obviously had to deal with some aspect of Indo-British relations and I immediately thought of Tipu Sultan, one of the most politically perceptive and tragic figures in modern history."[1]

The radio play was broadcast by the BBC on 15th August 1997 under the direction of Jatinder Verma of Tara Arts. Saeed Jaffrey played the lead role of Tipu Sultan. Later on, the play was rewritten as a stage play in English and then in Kannada. The Kannada version of this play was staged by the Karnataka Nataka Rangayan, Mysore in 1999 under the direction of C. Basavalingaiah in the precincts of Tipu's summer palace, Daria Daulat in Seringapatam on the 200th Death Anniversary of Tipu Sultan. It was first presented in English by the Madras Players at the YMCA Amphitheatre, Chennai, on 17th February 2000. This play was published by the Oxford University Press, New Delhi in 2004 as *Two Plays—The Dreams of Tipu Sultan* along with *Bali: The Sacrifice*.

The Dreams of Tipu Sultan deals with the early days of colonialism which centre round Tipu Sultan and his dreams in the last phase of his life. Using the facts of history, Karnad has deftly dramatized Tipu's struggle for emancipation. In his three historical plays, Karnad relates past events to those of the contemporary times, illustrating that history repeats itself in various ways and valuable lessons can be learnt from experience.

Aparna Dharwadker observes: "*The Dreams of Tipu Sultan* can be described as the long awaited history play in which Karnad confronts British colonialism in its crucial early stages of military expansion—paradoxically, at the invitation of the British, and for a celebration of Indian independence. The playwright notes that his 'obsession' with Tipu was something else he inherited from A.K. Ramanujan, who had begun but left unfinished a novel in English on the subject, and mentioned to him the secret diary in which Tipu had recorded his dreams. In 1987 Karnad located a copy of this diary at the University of Chicago's Regenstein Library.... When the B.B.C. approached Karnad in 1996 about a play relating to the independence theme, he 'didn't have to think twice' about the subject, and produced a work in which the impulse towards a complex poetic rehabilitation of Tipu is clearly evident."[2]

The Play's Theme and Story: Four Dreams of Tipu

In the play, Karnad highlights four dreams of Tipu recorded in his diary which emphasize his inner world and vision of life.

The play mainly concentrates on these dreams of Tipu in connection with the British power and their inroads into the country during Tipu's tenure. As a matter of fact, these dreams bring out the short-sightedness of the contemporary Indian rulers in understanding the real intention of the English and Tipu's serious concerns for the unity and integrity in the face of the British invasion. These dreams are very skilfully fused and flashbacked into the play.

Kirmani was once the most trusted person in the service of Tipu. He has now been appointed as a historian by the British. Mackenzie is very much interested to know the life and history of Tipu. Hence, he encourages Kirmani to write about

Tipu's administration and the subsequent fall of Seringapatam. However, Kirmani admits that writing about Tipu hurts him. He says, "There's no healing. True, the blood and tears dried up a long time ago. But the wound remains fresh" (181). This shows Kirmani's love and respect for Tipu. The way Tipu Sultan was destroyed by the English deeply hurts him. Kirmani spent his life in serving Tipu and his father Haidar Ali. And now he is in the service of the English, the arch-opponents of Tipu.

Now, the scene shifts to the battlefield. Captain Wilks and his soldiers are searching for the dead body of Tipu. At last, Nadeem Khan identifies the body of his Sultan. Wellesley expresses his joy after finding the body of Tipu, the "Tiger of Mysore". Unfortunately, the body of the Sultan is treated inhumanly by the English soldiers, as one of them disfigures it by cutting off one of Tipu's whiskers.

By using Kirmani and Mackenzie as *Sutradhars* of the play, Karnad reveals the different features of Tipu's personality projecting him as "one of the most politically perceptive and tragic figures in modern Indian history".[3]

The playwright takes us to the scene, where Tipu had his *first dream*—while returning with his army from Farrukhi near Salamabad. In this dream, Tipu is accompanied by Poornaiya, the Finance Minister. They come across a big temple in a dilapidated, ruined state. They watch strange figures in the temple. There are stone images moving their eyes. Of these images, two living women stand up and say that they have been seeking for their salvation through prayers; so, they need complete isolation. Tipu, at once, asks Poornaiya to get the temple repaired so that they can seek after God undisturbed. This act of Tipu clearly shows his respect for worship and his deep sense of secularism.

When Tipu and Poornaiya come out of the temple, they meet two old men who are the envoys of the Emperor of China. One of them informs Tipu that the Emperor of China has sent a white elephant and the horses as a symbol of friendship and affection for him. The old man further adds that "...the Emperor has never sent a white elephant to anyone except the Great Alexander and now to Your Presence" (194).

Tipu's interpretation of his own dream obviously suggests that he has a strong desire to be a powerful king in India. He knows well that the British who have come to India as traders will gradually capture the whole of India. So, he wants to thwart their wicked policy of 'Divide and Rule'. And their inroads upon the integrity of a country will be checkmated only when he becomes as powerful as Alexander. In order to drive the British out of India, Tipu tries to seek support from the local kings of neighbouring provinces by settling his differences with them. So, Tipu seems to be aware of his importance in the world history.

After this first dream, the scene of the play moves to the *Diwan-i-khas,* where we see Tipu holding a conference with Mir Sadiq and Poornaiya. Here, Tipu's dialogues reveal his great concern for the overall development of his kingdom of Mysore. He is well aware of the requirement and productivity of his state.

As far as trade and commerce is concerned, Tipu's knowledge of it seems to be remarkable. He is quick enough to imbibe the good habits and skill and economics cultivated by the English. It is because of his profound interest in trade and commerce, the English consider him, their staunch enemy.

As a father, he wants his sons Fath Haider, Muizuddin and Abdul Khaliq to listen carefully to his discussion on the state affairs with Osman Khan and Gulam Ali Khan. In the eighteenth century, Tipu was the only Indian king who tried to check the expansion of the English by making an alliance with the French. He sends his men Osman Khan and Gulam Ali Khan to consult the king of France and inform him about the situation in India, especially the condition of the French here. He also tells them to persuade the king, "if the French don't wake up, the English will gobble up the whole of India. The French here have become listless. The King must prod them, kick them if necessary into activity" (198).

Tipu has a strong desire to defeat the English by signing a treaty with the French. He firmly asserts that if he has ten thousand French soldiers, he will certainly change the face of India. He is conscious of the increasing power of the English in India. Therefore, he wants weapons and armed forces to face the British invasion in his state.

But Tipu is quite sure of the fact that these neighbouring countries cannot be friends forever and they will soon start quarrelling. Tipu is clever enough to know that the British have appointed Lord Cornwallis as the Governor General of India to create furore in the country. He rightly guesses that Cornwallis, after his defeat in America by Washington, will try his best to get the stain off his reputation by defeating him.

The second dream of Tipu as presented in the play reveals his nationalistic spirit. Tipu sincerely thinks that all the rulers of the country should come together to hinder the progress of the British imperialism in India. The Marathas and the Nizam are the neighbouring rulers of Tipu's kingdom. Though they are his enemies, Tipu sincerely tries to mobilize them to fight against the British. However, his sincere efforts of bringing them together prove to be futile. The British, very cunningly succeed in dividing the Indian rulers by exploiting their policy of 'Divide and Rule'. They systematically split these southern kingdoms and by making an opportunistic alliance with the Marathas and the Nizam, they succeed in defeating Tipu Sultan.

In the next scene, we find the Maratha Court in Pune, where Nana Phadnavis, the Maratha statesman is talking with Charles Malet, representative of Lord Cornwallis. Malet tries to convince Nana that the English are the good friends of the Marathas. Nana suspects the hidden intentions of the English. But in the meanwhile, crafty strategy of Malet works out and Nana responds to Malet's proposal of friendship.

By using the historical facts, Karnad skilfully throws light on the contemporary political situation. Malet's request of Nana to support the British in declaring war against Tipu reminds us of George Bush, the former American President, requesting the world to support him in his campaign against terrorism, which America herself has initiated.

Tipu's men insist that they should declare war against the English as the terms dictated are completely unfair and grossly cruel. However, Tipu decides to accept their demands as he does not want the destruction of his city. So, there is no other choice left before Tipu except accepting their demands. The British ask Tipu to exchange his sons for his kingdom.

In the third dream, Tipu's father, Haidar Ali has come to him. It is a painful scene in which his dead father reprimands him seriously for the losses: "You have maimed me, Tipu. You have cut off my limbs and handed them over to the enemy" (224).

The dream has symbolic significance. Tipu returns the territories which his father has won from the Marathas. Tipu's father holds him responsible for allowing Cornwallis' escape. What Tipu tells his father in the dream becomes his own vision and ambition to be powerful like them and make his country as a whole, united, nation quite similar to the English.

Tipu's prediction comes true. Later on, both the Marathas and the Nizam are deceived by the English. Tipu, after some years, decides to accept the policy "to use a thorn to take out the thorn". As a part of this strategy, he plans to accept the conditions of the English. Tipu thinks that by accepting their terms, he can throw their whole strategy into confusion. But his followers insist that instead of accepting the terms they will fight to the finish. But in reality all his noble men turn out as traitors.

In the role of *sutradhar*, Kirmani narrates how the English besieged the fort of Seringapatam on 4th May 1799. That very night, Tipu sees his fourth dream. In his dream, he sees that everyone is reporting him about the good things taking place in the favour of his state. His son Haider informs him that their soldiers are ready to attack. Mir Sadiq comes with good news telling that the Nizam has realized his mistake in supporting the English. Likewise, the Marathas also have decided to help Tipu. Qilledar Nadeem Khan tells him that Hari Pant Phadke is waiting to have a word with him.

Tipu is confident that with the help of the Marathas and the Nizam, they will certainly defeat the English at any time. Poornaiya admires the Sultan for his dynamic leadership and the prophetic vision of the future. Tipu orders to call the entire *zanana* out to celebrate the victory. This is the last dream of Tipu. The dream cannot be transformed into reality. Tipu is killed in the battle.

Commenting on the last dream of Tipu, Aparna Dharwadker, remarks, "The last dream is the most poignant because it is a fantasy of victory in the midst of defeat and death. The insertion of this dream-text into history introduces a level of experience even more evanescent than memory, and makes the *Dreams of Tipu Sultan* Karnad's most poetic play.[4]

Critical Interpretation and Appraisal of the Play

The play is divided into two acts. There is continuous shifting between the dream and reality. Though there is no mention of the scenes, there are, in fact, many scenes in the play. They change from one place to another and from one period of time to another. The time changes from the present to the past and vice versa.

There are several characters in the play besides the protagonist Tipu Sultan, the eighteenth-century ruler in the western Karnataka. They are Ruqayya Banu, Tipu's most loving queen; Poornaiya, his Finance Minister; Mir Sadiq, his commander-at-arms; Lord Cornwallis, Richard Wellesley (Earl of Mornington), the Governor General of India; and his younger brother Arthur Wellesley; Col. William Kirkpatrick, Charles Malet, the representative of Cornwallis and the historians Hussain Ali Khan Kirmani and Col. Colin Mackenzie, the Oriental Scholar.

Throughout the play, the two historians, just mentioned, play a role of *sutradhara* similar to the tradition of the classical Sanskrit plays and the folk theatre structure. It is important to note how historical events and characters in the play come alive and fresh with the artistic touch of Karnad. Expressing her views on Karnad's artistic skill of merging historical facts with fictional elements, Aparna Dharwadker aptly points out:

> Karnad interlineates 'textualised' history with legend, lore, and memory because all these modes of transmission are germane to the story of Tipu. The ruler's fabled persona as the Tiger of Mysore thus figures prominently in the action, both as oral legend and as a military reality that the English must contend with.[5]

And further she observes how Karnad quite successfully portrays the character of Tipu throwing light on his multi-faceted roles. She continues:

> Karnad also casts his protagonist in multiple and contradictory roles—as a beloved ruler, legendary warrior, loving father, and visionary dreamer, but also as he Machiavellian schemer who plots with the French against the English, the defeated soldier who enters into humiliating treaties with the enemy, and the gullible commander who is eventually betrayed by his own side. [6]

The play moves on with the arguments of the two historians Hussain Ali Khan Kirmani and Col. Colin Mackenzie, the Oriental Scholar of the history of Tipu, his controversial agreement with the French and his record of dreams. The play dangles round the present and the past. Both the historians discuss Tipu's past life: how he lived and what he strongly desired for, and how he saw the dreams which he recorded in his notebook along with his own interpretations of them. The history of Tipu is thus revealed in the first scene of the play.

The action of the play takes place in 1803, four years after Tipu's death on the battlefield on 4th May 1799 at Seringapatam. The play also concludes with the historians' discussion over the last battle which was ultimately won by the British due to the treachery of Tipu's trusted officers and the neighbouring kings.

Major historical events associated with Tipu's life, his ruling, his benevolent attitude towards his Hindu subjects, his fascination for importing technologies and technicians from foreign countries, his admiration for Europeans' trading skill and their zeal and zest to capture the whole world and his last fight against the English have been graphically dramatized by the playwright. In between are the flashes of the Sultan's dreams, which he himself had carefully recorded and interpreted. While talking to Tutun Mukherjee, Karnad refers to the dreams of Tipu Sultan. He says:

> What I find fascinating is the fact that Tipu Sultan, who practically spent forty-nine years of his life on horseback, recorded his dreams and kept them under his pillow, I

> wondered whether those dreams dictated his actions. It is, of course, a greater marvel that the notebook survived the ravages of time. This was a historical curiosity, I thought, that had to be highlighted.[7]

Karnad has added a postscript to this play in which the tragedy of Tipu's successors is ironically described. In this way, *The Dreams of Tipu Sultan* brings out the tragedy of the Tiger of Mysore who sensed the advent of colonialism with the arrival of the English in the garb of traders. Tipu did his best to unite his neighbouring states but the English became successful in weakening the power of Indian kings with their policy of 'Divide and Rule'. In this regard, Aparna Dharwadker aptly says:

> Karnad's principal thematic argument is a familiar one: the English succeeded in India not only (or even principally) because of their superior weapons and warfare, but because of their ability to play off the members of the native ruling elite against each other.[8]

Conclusion

To sum up, Karnad uses the facts from history and narrates the four dreams of Tipu, and, thereby, connects the past with the present. He portrays him as the ideal kings who tries to bring unity and equality in the society. His principles of unity and integrity of the country are even more significant in the present context. One important thing to note is that narrating a factual history on the stage is not the purpose of Karnad's dramatic art. The factual history becomes a sort of social and political myth or fantasy of the present century in the hands of Karnad. Thus, his interpretation of history bears relevance to the contemporary times and the zeitgeist, that is the spirit of the age. Karnad's history plays—*Tughlaq, Tale-Danda,* and *The Dreams of Tipu Sultan* seem to mirror the same reality and carry the same message.

Notes

1. Girish Karnad, *Appendix*-2. "Note on *The Dreams of Tipu Sultan.*" *Collected Plays*. Volume Two. New Delhi: OUP, 2005, 303.

2. Aparna Dharwadker, "Introduction". *Collected Plays. op. cit.*, xxii-xxiii.
3. Girish Karnad, *Appendix*-2. *op. cit.*, 303.
4. Aparna Dharwadker, "Introduction". *Collected Plays. op. cit.*, xxvi.
5. *Ibid.*, xxiv.
6. *Ibid.*
7. Tutun Mukherjee, "In His Own Voice: A Conversation with Girish Karnad". *Girish Karnad's Plays: Performance and Critical Perspectives*. Delhi: Pencraft International, 2006, 48.
8. Aparna Dharwadker, "Introduction". *Collected Plays. op. cit.*, xxv.

FOLK PLAYS

8

Hayavadana: Quest for Completeness

Introduction

Indian theatre has the three-fold tradition: the classical/Sanskrit, the folk, and the modern. It is best manifested in Karnad's plays. His plays are based on Indian history, myth, and folk-tale. The Karnad theatre has an intimate link with its roots in the classical and the folk traditions. However, it is noticed that he made use of culture to destroy its own false values. That is why in "Author's Introduction" to the *Three Plays* he states: "The energy of folk theatre comes from the fact that although it seems to uphold traditional values, it also has the means of questioning these values, of making them literally stand on their head."[1]

Although the plays are based on the traditional myths, folk-tales or history, they are modern since the issues raised in them belong to all times and climes. Through his plays, Karnad portrays modern man's anguish and dilemma in a hostile situation. The play *Hayavadana* deals with the theme of incompleteness. It is depicted through the character of horse-headed man Hayavadana after whom the play is titled. According to K. Narasimha Murthy, "*Hayavadana* is a Brechtian kind of play employing native folk theatre strategies to present, through a folk-tale, man's tragically futile aspiration for perfection."[2]

The central episode in the play—the story of Devadatta and Kapila is based on a tale in *Kathasaritasagar*, a collection of stories in Sanskrit and on Thomas Mann's German novella *The Transposed Heads*. While pointing out the importance of the play, Erin B. Mee states: "*Hayavadana*'s origins are intergeneric—a folk tale transformed into a novella into a play—and intercultural—the story has travelled from India to Germany and back again. 'Inter-ness' pervades *Hayavadana* at every level, from its origins to its thematic content, to its production history."[3]

The Play's Theme and Story

The play has two plots: The main plot describes the life story of the two friends: Kapila and Devadatta and the sub-plot depicts the story of the eponymous character Hayavadana. Both the plots develop simultaneously and deal with the same theme of physical deformity caused by the schism between the mind and the body. This theme is hinted at the very outset: Like the Sanskrit/classical play, the play starts with an invocation to Lord Ganesha "The choice of elephant-headed God is significant as Lord Ganesha with human body and animal head aptly suggests the central theme of incompleteness of being."[4] As Bhagavata says: "An elephant's head on a human body, a broken tusk and a cracked belly—whichever way you look at him, he seems the embodiment of imperfection, of incompleteness. How indeed can one fathom the mystery that this very Vakratunda-Mahakaya, with his crooked face and distorted body, is the Lord of Success and Perfection?" (105-06). As Bhagavata starts narrating the story and introducing the main characters, Hayavadana arrives on the stage. Like Ganesha, Hayavadana, the horse-headed man, also suggests physical deformity. His present state is the result of his mother's marriage with a stallion, a cursed Gandharva. He has been trying to become complete by performing various religious and social services. On Bhagavata's advice, he goes to the Goddess Kali to seek her blessings.

With the exit of Hayavadana, the main plot of the play begins. It is the story of friendship of Devadatta and Kapila. Devadatta is a Brahmin and Kapila, a blacksmith. Devadatta, as per his academic status, spends most of his time in reading and writing. In doing so, he neglects his body completely. He has made his mark as a scholar, since he writes excellent poetry and defeats several scholars in discussions. Kapila has his own identity. Just as Devadatta is the master of learning, he is an adept in sports. He plays games and often participates in sports. He defeats many wrestlers in competitions. However, he develops his body and neglects his mind. Thus, describing their friendship, the playwright remarks: "Two friends there were—one mind, one heart" (106).

Karnad here exposes a hierarchical structure of the Indian society in which the Brahmins are on the highest pedestal. It is for this reason that Devadatta is always presented sitting on a chair and Kapila on the floor.

In achieving their cherished goals in learning and sports, Devadatta neglects his body and Kapila his mind. It is due to this incompleteness that Devadatta falls in love fifteen times but fails to marry any of the girls. "Kapila cannot perceive the bodily sensation of love as his mind is not nimble but he has the initiative and arranges things easily as his body is agile."[5] Devadatta is quite aware of it. So, he makes a friendly appeal to Kapila to help him convert his love for Padmini into marriage. While expressing the intensity of his heart, he says to Kapila: "I swear, Kapila, with you as my witness, if I ever get her as my wife, I'll sacrifice my two arms to the goddess Kali, I'll sacrifice my head to Lord Rudra" (120).

Kapila succeeds in arranging Devadatta's marriage to Padmini. But he is rather suspicious as to whether Devadatta, with his frail body can be a successful life-companion for Padmini. He (Kapila) says to himself: "But this one is fast as lighting and as sharp. She is not for the likes of you. What she needs is a man of steel" (126). Thus, he, too, expresses his love for her.

The rest of the play focuses on Padmini. In their trip to Ujjain, she gets fascinated by Kapila. Devadatta cannot bear Padmini gazing at Kapila with love. In a fit of jealousy, he goes to the temple of Kali and cuts off his own head. Kapila finds the dead body and thinking rationally that he will be blamed for Devadatta's suicide, he also beheads himself. Padmini is about to follow the beaten track with a view that there may be definitely a terrified gossip and she will be held guilty for these suicides. Goddess Kali appears on the scene and agrees to restore the dead to life. She unveils to Padmini the hypocrisy of the friends and asks her to put the heads back on their bodies. But

Padmini, with her strong, intense desire to possess the man of her dreams—the one with Devadatta's mind and Kapila's body—transposes their heads. "Devadatta and Kapila are revived with their heads transposed."[6] So, the question arises: Which of the two is her husband, the one with Devadatta's head or the one with his body? A great sage, explaining the *shastras*, suggests a remedy that the head is considered the supreme part of the body, and hence, the man with Devadatta's head is, therefore, her husband. Thus, Padmini's innate desire gets fulfilled. Now, she has a complete man who is supreme in mind and body. She is quite happy to go home with the new Devadatta and Kapila then begins to live a life of a recluse in the forest.

But the desired changes remain temporary. Padmini sends Devadatta again to the trip to Ujjain after some years, and in his absence, she goes to Kapila along with her little child. In the course of time, Devadatta arrives at the place. A duel takes place between the friends, turned to rivals, which ultimately leads to their death. Giving the responsibility of her child to the Bhagavata to be handed over to his grandfather at the age of five, Padmini commits *sati*. She dies with a longing to possess a complete man.

The son neither laughs nor weeps. Meanwhile, Hayavadana returns there as a complete horse but with a human voice. When Padmini's son sees Hayavadana and listens to him singing a patriotic song, he sheds his gloom and starts laughing and clapping his hands. Hayavadana's singing ends up as a proper neigh and, thus, he loses his human voice. In this way, getting over their disabilities, both Hayavadana and the child become all right and, thus, complete. Padmini's desire is thereby fulfilled. With the curtain raised, all the three are shown as coming alive in flesh and blood. Like the beginning, the play ends again with their prayer to the Lord Ganesha. Thus, what the play demands of its audience is "willing suspension of disbelief" to use Coleridge's words.

Critical Interpretation and Appraisal of the Play

Hayavadana, a play in two acts, is Karnad's third play which was originally written in Kannada in 1970 and later on translated into English by the playwright himself in 1971. Immediately in 1972, it won both the annual Sangeet Natak Akademi Award and the Kamaladevi Award of the Bharatiya Natak Sangh as the best Indian play.

The play is based on a story from a collection of tales titled *Kathasagara* and the further development of this story by Thomas Mann in a novella titled *The Transposed Heads*. The use of mask has various dimensions in the play. It represents a contrast in reality and appearance, i.e. the fact and the pretence. Karnad himself states: "Western theatre has developed a contrast between the *face* and the *mask*—the real inner person and the exterior one presents, or wishes to present, to the world outside."[7] Lord Ganesha, the elephant-headed God also has the mask of elephant. Although Ganesha ensures successful completion of any endeavour, for Karnad, this Vakratunda-Mahakaya is the symbol of physical deformity. Another idea that is presented through the play is that the head represents the cognitive aspects of man, the intellect. That is why Hayavadana becomes a complete horse towards the end of the play.

According to Suman B. Bala, "The sub-plot of *Hayavadana* the horse-headed man...deepens the significance of the main theme of incompleteness by treating it on a different plane. It provides the framework of the play both as a prologue and as an epilogue."[8] As Krishna Gandhi writes, "The theme of the play is an old one...man's yearning for completeness, for perfection. It's this yearning which makes people restless in their ordinary existence, and makes them reach out for extraordinary things.... But the ideal of perfection itself is ambiguous. The character of Hayavadana is invented as an example of this ambiguity."[9]

Karnad has given a very subtle treatment to the twin aspects of life: love and sex. It is Kapila who performs the marriage of Padmini and Devadatta. But Padmini's love for Kapila can be noticed from the very first incident when they meet each other. Right from the beginning, she seems to be in love of Kapila also. That is why he said, "What she needs is a man of steel" (126). In his marital life, Devadatta also becomes aware of Padmini's being enamoured of Kapila. Both of them love her but they put on the mask of friendship and conceal their real love and passion. Padmini is very shrewd, dynamic, rational and genius. Like Devadatta and Kapila, she is not hypocritical. That is why she transposes the heads and gets her secret desire fulfilled. The sexual connotations are too lucid to remain concealed. It is revealed when Kapila climbs the tree to get the Fortunate Lady Flowers for Padmini. Devadatta himself admits: "No woman would resist him—and what does it matter that she is married" (134). Towards the end of the play, Padmini again arouses in Kapila a passion for sexual pleasure. It is made clear through the description: "Kapila raises his head and looks at her. She caresses his face, like a blind person trying to imprint it on her finger tips. Then, she rests her head on his chest.... Kapila lifts her up and takes her in" (171). Karnad represents their meeting and mating through the images of water, waterfall and rain that is found in Sanskrit plays. Padmini spends five days in the company of Kapila and enjoys the pure delight born of the physical union with the man she has been longing for. "Her menacing voyage to reach a longed for heaven involves fulfilment of desire and death. Padmini's premonition is tragically accurate; she knows the limit of erotic ecstasy is death."[10]

Through the character of Padmini, Karnad portrays a "new woman" who is free and has no hitch or hesitation in sharing the emotional, if not conjugal, lives of the two men. Throughout the play, it is she who controls the situation and moulds the men to behave according to her wishes and aspirations. She is rational and determined. However, she gets defeated by the forces of nature. According to Suman Bala, "Padmini's predicament is the predicament of a modern, emancipated woman in our society, who is born between two polarities, a woman who loves her husband as well as someone else for two different aspects of their personalities. Padmini is fascinated by both Devadatta and Kapila and this creates the problem. The two men cannot accept each other when it comes to sharing a woman and all the three destroy themselves in the process."[11]

The central problem of incompleteness leads to identity crisis. It is related to Padmini in the main plot and Hayavadana in the sub-plot. In Padmini's case, the cause of identity crisis is her search for complete man. She wants to possess a perfect man with a scholarly mind like Devadatta's and muscular figure like Kapila's. Opportunity comes in the form of Kali's grant of boons. She transposes the heads of the dead bodies of Devadatta and Kapila and fulfils her desire. However, the desired changes vanish in the course of time and, again, she has her previous companion, i.e. a scholar with a weak frame. Her attraction for Kapila always remains ever green. So, in Devadatta's absence, she goes to the forest to live with Kapila Expressing her agony, she says: "Yes, you won, Kapila. Devadatta won, too. But I—the better half of two bodies—I neither win nor lose" (170). Devadatta arrives there and puts an end to their unsettled triangular life. Devadatta dies and with him Kapila, too, with their identities kept intact as a scholar and a wrestler, respectively. But Padmini has no identity. In the second half of the play, she lives with a man who has Kapila's body and Devadatta's head. So the question arises, whose wife is she? While performing *sati*, she remarks:

> Kali, Mother of all Nature, you must have your joke even now. Other women can die praying that they should get the same husband in all the lives to come. You haven't left me even that consolation. (177)

And that is woman's tragic fate.

Hayavadana faces the problem of identity crisis throughout the play: To which community or species does he belong? But the problem is solved at the end of the play. With Kali's blessings, he becomes a complete horse and also receives his voice of horse later on. Being an animal, he is free from physical deformity. P. Dhanavel justifiably states: "The play reveals the essential ambiguity of human personality which is apparently shaped or shattered by the human environment. Fundamentally incomplete and imperfect, the human beings search and strive for attaining the unattainable ideal of completeness and perfection.... The best solution for the identity crisis...is reconciliation with one's own self and the environment."[12]

The Bhagavata's role is similar to that of the *sutradhara* in the Sanskrit plays or the chorus in the Greek plays. He narrates the story, introduces the major characters in the play, provides the connecting links in the action, informs the audiences about major developments such as the marriage of Devadatta and Padmini in Act I, the *rishi's* verdict on the problem of the transposed heads in Act II. He passes comments on the characters which throw light on the innermost thoughts of the major characters. Similarly, he seems to play the role of a minor character in the action, as it is he who tells Devadatta where Kapila lives in the forest. Like the chorus, he is found signalling the time between the two acts by telling the audience, "There's a break of ten minutes now. Please have some tea, ponder over the situation and come back with your solutions. We shall then continue with our enquiry" (149). This is in keeping with the play's Breachtian technique of "Alienation Effect". And the play ends with his benedictory final prayer which is similar to the *Bharatavakya* of an ancient Sanskrit drama. M.K. Naik states: "In fact, the final, transitional benedictory prayer, after invoking divine help in the cause of general prosperity as usual, ends with an unorthodox, ironical touch: Give the rulers of our country success in all endeavours and along with it, a little bit of sense" (186). And since Hayavadana, now a complete horse, stands by the side of the Bhagavata as he sends the prayer, the kind of sense required is also appropriately suggested. This sudden dovetailing of the ancient and the modern emphasizes "how an ancient fable can have urgent relevance to our own age."[13]

Like the Bhagavata, the female chorus and the dolls also perform the role of the *sutradhara* very effectively. The dolls also provide commentary on the changing situation in the second half of the play. They throw light on the secrets of Padmini's mind. They report Devadatta's transformation back to his earlier, original self.

Conclusion

The play *Hayavadana* has an intimate link with the classical and the folk theatre. Like the classical Sanskrit play, it begins with a *nandi*, i.e. a prayer to Lord Ganesha. It has a ritualistic function as the characters here pray God to assist them in the successful performance of the play. Apart from this ritualistic function, it throws light on the theme of the play. Karnad has used this device very skilfully for Lord Ganesha with his human body and elephant head aptly suggests the central theme of incompleteness of man's life.

To sum up, in *Hayavadana*, Karnad condenses several themes into the plot of the play and enriches it with cultural significance.[14] The elements in Sanskrit theatre such as *nandi*, the role of *sutradhara*, and that of the folk theatre such as *Yakshagana, Kathkali* have been used very effectively. "In the opening scene, Bhagavata, the actor, and the female chorus assemble on the stage and announce the theme to be played in the popular folk modes of *Rosadhari* and *Khayals*."[15] The play has a rich variety of themes such as (i) quest for identity, (ii) incompleteness, (iii) love, marriage, and sex, (iv) mind and body dichotomy, (v) social system and social norms, etc. The play is sublime and universal and has set a high water-mark of dramatics and dramaturgy. To conclude it, in the words of P. Dhanavel, "The play flows like an underground river that springs out in different directions yet remains a forceful and vigourous current reaching out to the sea of human experiences."[16]

Notes

1. Girish Karnad, "Author's Introduction". *Three Plays*. Delhi: OUP, 1994, 14.
2. K. Narasimha Murthy, *Modern Kannada Literature*. Bangalore: Pustakalaya Publications, 1992. Quoted in Suman Bala, "This Mad Dance of Incompleteness: Search for Completeness in Girish Karnad's *Hayavadana*". *New Directions in Indian Drama*. Ed. Sudhakar Pandey and Freya Barua. New Delhi: Prestige, 1994, 165.
3. Erin B. Mee, "*Hayavadana*: Model of Complexity." *Girish Karnad's Plays Performance and Critical Perspectives*. Ed. Tutun Mukherjee. New Delhi: Pencraft International, 2006, 149.
4. Suman Bala, "This Mad Dance of Incompleteness: Search for Completeness in Girish Karnad's *Hayavadana*". *New Directions in Indian Drama*. *op. cit.*, 165.
5. Manchi Sarat Babu, *Indian Drama Today: A Study in the Theme of Cultural Deformity*. Bombay: Prestige, 1997, 85.
6. Borrowed from Thomas Mann's *The Transposed Heads*. A modified and elaborated version of the sixth story of *Vetala Panchavimsati*. Quoted in Manchi, Sarat Babu. *op. cit.*, 85.

7. Girish Karnad, "Appendix 1". *Collected Plays*. Vol. 1. New Delhi: OUP, 2005, 312.
8. Suman Bala, *op. cit.*, 166.
9. Krishna Gandhi, "*Hayavadana*", *Enact*, 68-69 (Aug.-Sept. 1972) n.p. Quoted in Suman Bala. *op. cit.*, 166.
10. Vanashree Tripathi, "*Hayavadana*: Towards Forging an Indian Theatre". *Three Plays of Girish Karnad: A Study in Poetics and Culture*. New Delhi: Prestige, 2004, 56.
11. Suman Bala, *op. cit.*, 174.
12. P. Dhanavel, *The Indian Imagination of Girish Karnad*. New Delhi: Prestige, 2000, 47.
13. M.K. Naik, "From the Horse's Mouth: A Study of *Hayavadana*". *Girish Karnad's Plays: Performance and Critical Perspectives*. *op. cit.*, 143.
14. P. Dhanavel, *op. cit.*, 73.
15. Vanashree Tripathi, *op. cit.*, 50.
16. P. Dhanavel, *op. cit.*, 74.

9

Nagamandala: Gender Consciousness

Introduction

Girish Karnad experiments with new forms and techniques in the structure of his plays. As he explains in an interview on receiving the Jnanpith Award, "I cannot invent plots; therefore, I use myths. I cannot invent stories and hence go to history."[1] The play *Nagamandala* subtitled *A Play with a Cobra* is based upon a folklore story. Outwardly, the play appears simple but in it, Karnad has successfully co-ordinated the elements of myth, magic, folk belief, and romance. The play starts with a prologue which effectively sets the tone and mood of the play.

The Play's Theme and Story

The play opens in a surrealistic setting: the inner sanctum of a ruined temple. The idol is broken. So, the presiding deity of the temple cannot be identified. It is night. Moonlight seeps in through the cracks in the roof and the walls. A man, suspended between life and death, is sitting in this temple. He is cursed for making his audience fall asleep twisted in miserable chairs, who came trusting him. "All that abused mass of sleep has turned against him and become the cause of Death" (247). That is the last night of his life, if he fails to keep himself awake all through the night by telling a story.

Meanwhile Flames and Story arrive in the temple to share some gossip. Man requests the Story to tell him a tale accepting her condition that "he will tell it again to someone else" (252). This is the Breachtian technique of "Alienation-Effect", very favourite with Girish Karnad, the veteran playwright.

It is a story of Rani whose husband enjoys extra-marital sex with a concubine, openly and unashamedly, and locks Rani in his absence. He is reluctant to spend time with her. An old woman, Kurudavva, a friend of Appanna's mother, is greatly moved by Rani's plight. She gives her a medicinal root to fascinate her husband. On the advice of Kurudavva, Rani mixes the root in the food and cooks it. The solution appears like blood. Thinking that it may be poisonous and can cause a serious harm to her husband, Rani throws it off. Incidentally, it falls upon an anthill within which lived Naga, the King Cobra. Getting affected by the love potion, he falls in love with Rani. He starts visiting Rani every night, assuming the form of Appanna, her husband. That is role-shifting, in short. May be, psychologically speaking, that Naga is Appana's alter ego. In the beginning, Rani is somewhat shocked due to her husband's rudeness during the day and amorousness in the night. However, in course of time, she learns to accept it and enjoy it. The conjugal love results ultimately in her pregnancy. When Rani informs Naga that she is pregnant, he gets anxious for her and tells her to follow his directions in toto and without fail. Rani's husband Appanna discovers her pregnancy. He is sure that she has committed adultery as he has never been in bed with her. The village elders ask Rani to prove her chastity by giving an ordeal. As per the suggestions of Naga, Rani offers to go through a "snake ordeal". She thrusts her hand into the anthill, pulls out the venomous King Cobra. She swears that she has never touched anybody except her husband and the Cobra. Naga spreads his hood over her head, sways it for a while, coils himself round her neck like a garland and goes away. The whole village acclaims her 'a goddess incarnate' and her husband is forced to accept her as such. Appanna falls at her feet and begs for her forgiveness. Now, he is her devoted husband and his concubine becomes her maid-servant. However, Rani's acceptance by her husband has tragic consequences for Naga. He cannot visit Rani any longer. As he cannot live without her, he entangles himself in her hair and commits suicide. Rani now gets conscious of the mystery. She honours Naga's supreme sacrifice by making her son (born of him) light his funeral pyre in accordance with the religious practice. Thus, the story may be cited as the best example of what Coleridge calls "willing suspension of disbelief".

Critical Interpretation and Appraisal of the Play

The title of the play is highly symbolic: "Naga" stands for the character of the King Cobra and a "mandala" for the triangular relationship of Rani, her husband and her lover. "Mandala" may be seen as the four sides of the square providing the dramatic framework, viz. the Flames (the observer), the Story (the play's plot), the Man (the playwright) and the audience (the respondees). Rani's appearance on the stage throughout the play adds to the feministic aura of the play.[2]

According to Girish Karnad, "Appanna and Naga represent the two unconnected roles of a husband as a stranger during the day and as lover at night."[3] Rajinder Paul rightly points out: "It is a play where a cobra plays the lover and proves to be better behaved than his human counterpart who is as insensitive as a husband as we read about in bad tales."[4]

The society projected in the play is divided on the basis of gender. The play is a critique of the gender-biased values and mores of the patriarchal society, where women have been oppressed for centuries. On the day of her trial, Rani has been asked to prove her chastity by giving an ordeal, while Appanna goes unquestioned, even unnoticed. Appanna enjoys extra-marital relationship quite openly with the concubine and tries to punish Rani severely for the same even when she is unconscious or ignorant of the sin of adultery. Thus, the play exposes the double standards of this so-called cultured society that strongly demands of a woman the fidelity to her husband but not of a man the constancy of love for his wife. In the Indian society, fidelity is expected only from a woman and man is left scot-free to commit sins. That is why the village elders ask Rani alone to prove her fidelity.

As mentioned earlier, Naganna is the alter ego of Appanna. Appanna and Naganna are actually the two appearances of man's nature: the one, seen during the day, who performs the role of a dictator, and the other, at night who plays the lover's role. These two contradictory faces symbolize a woman's exploitation by man and his double standards of morality. Rani symbolizes woman's endless suffering in the male-dominated society.

However, the forces of love prevail over those of tyranny. That is why Rani is helped by the King Cobra. She is not only rid of the trap but is also honoured and worshipped by the society around. So, B.T. Seetha is quite justified in pointing out: "If *Nagamandala* symbolizes a woman's predicament in a traditional...family set-up, there is also an underlying metaphor of love that rises from the realms of an abyss to reach the heights of a sanctified relationship of acceptance and reverence."[5] Rani and Appanna are presented as a couple who 'lived happily ever after', though not without a sense of restlessness as reflected in Appanna's inability to comprehend Rani's motherhood and her status as a goddess and Rani's anguish to know whether it was her husband or a third person, that came to her as the lover.

In the Indian society, marriage is considered to be the holiest of holy institutions. It is believed that fidelity of a woman to her husband is the way to her salvation. Chastity is looked upon as supreme virtue which she is expected to protect at the cost of her life. Rani is the true symbol of woman's piety and endurance. She is married in her teens; in the course of years, she grows physically mature. Because of her husband's apathy towards her, she behaves like a scared child in her new home. In the company of Naga, she is happy, for it is he who makes love to her and offers her enjoyment and knowledge of the world.

Towards the end of the play, Rani is portrayed as a goddess. But she never dreams of such a divine image. Throughout the play, she appears earthy and human. That is why the very realization, that she is going to be a mother, gives her joy. There is a definite shift in her character. The play depicts her journey from an innocent, helpless, vulnerable, ignorant girl into a confident, courageous, clever, determined, and self-assertive lady. It is evident, when she says, "I was a stupid, ignorant girl when you brought me here. But now I am a woman, a wife, and I am going to be a mother" (283-84). After undertaking the snake ordeal, she receives what she has been longing for, i.e. her husband's love and affection. However, her union with her true husband results in a cessation of her love relationship with Naga, who can neither renounce his passion for her nor kill her. So, he commits suicide. Now, Rani is clever enough to realize the fact and to manipulate/maneuver the situation accordingly. V. Rangan justifiably points out, "By the end of the play, Rani has travelled a long route from innocence to experience. When she finds the dead Naga in her hair, she has acquired enough cunning to successfully persuade her husband to allow her son to perform the last rites for Naga, as a father is entitled to receive from his son."[6]

The snake ordeal, Rani undergoes, proves her purity which is actually an illusion. The fact is: Appanna has never shared bed with Rani. Naturally, he is not the father of the child, Rani has given birth to. Yet, he accepts both Rani and the child and hails Rani as goddess at the instance of the village-folk. He thinks that he is a sinner who has set the goddess on torture. So, he says: "Have I sinned so much that even Nature should laugh at me?" (294).

Conclusion

The play, thus, explores the dichotomy between truth and illusion. Rani, Naga, and Appanna are well aware of the facts. Still, all of them treat illusion as reality. Actually, each of them sees and perceives the truth from his/her own perspective. In the snake ordeal, Rani is speaking out the truth when she claims that she has touched only the two—her husband and the King Cobra. Naga gives her the protection by raising his hood over her head. Appanna's plea is that he has not touched his wife. So, the successful snake ordeal leaves him dumb-founded. The villagers, however, think that Rani is not just a woman but a goddess. First, Appanna wants to prove the truth but then prefers illusion to reality, believing that Nature has turned back upon him. Rani's innocence ends with the snake ordeal since she realizes another truth regarding the father of her child. Hers is a journey from ignorance to experience.

V. Rangan appropriately states: "Does *Nagamandala*... mean the 'coils of the cobra' that entangles Rani or is it Naga himself caught in the coils of love for Rani? Sex seems to be the road to salvation in the Karnad canon and holds an important place in all his plays.... It is the supreme path that teaches the lessons of life to Rani, Naga and Appanna."[7]

The folk-tale used in the play has several dimensions. Rani is innocent; she is ignorant of the adultery she commits. She suspects neither overtly nor covertly Naga's identity till the play's end. She must be either too innocent or too clever.

The 'Man' plays the role similar to that of the chorus in a Greek play. He is the *sutradhara* who introduces the main characters, supervises and passes comments on them, and correlates the events. Similarly, at the very outset of the play, there is a hint symbolically given about the nature of the play in these words: "The inner sanctum of a ruined temple. The idol is broken, so the presiding deity of the temple cannot be identified" (247). The ruined temple implies our world in shambles and the broken idol symbolizes "the fractured self"[8] of both—the husband and the wife. The King Cobra loses his identity in the love affair. He gets entangled in the throes of love. Towards the play's end, his relationship with Rani is a pleasing pain or sweet agony for him. A rival in love as he is, he cannot bear to see Rani, his beloved, in the arms of her husband. So, he decides to bite her. But he fails to do it since he himself states: "No, I can't. My love has stitched up my lips. Pulled out my fangs. Torn out of my sac of poison.... Yes, King Cobra is now no better than a grass snake" (296). This is how Karnad humanizes the King Cobra, as Milton does Satan in *Paradise Lost*. The pride and poison of the King Cobra have been subdued by Rani's love and affection. However, in the matter of love, he prevails upon both Appanna and Rani by sacrificing his life for Rani's marital bliss.

Notes

1. Quoted in B.T. Seetha, "Quest for Completeness in *Hayavadana* and *Nagamandala*." *Girish Karnad's Plays: Performance and Critical Perspectives*. Ed. Tutun Mukherjee. New Delhi: Pencraft International, 2006, 188.
2. V. Rangan, "Myth and Romance in *Nagamandala* or their Subversion?" *Girish Karnad's Plays Performance and Critical Perspectives. op. cit.*, 201.

3. Girish Karnad, "Author's Introduction". *Three Plays*. Delhi: OUP, 1994, 17.
4. *Ibid*.
5. B.T. Seetha, "Quest for Completeness in *Hayavadana* and *Nagamandala*". *op. cit*., 196.
6. V. Rangan, *op. cit*., 206.
7. *Ibid*.
8. B.T. Seetha, *op. cit*., 192.

10

Flowers: Listening to Soul

Introduction

The dramatic monologue *Flowers* by Karnad indicates his continuity of earlier themes and a departure from them as well in the sense that it is based on a folk-tale from the Chitradurga region of Karnataka, which fundamentally deals with the metaphysical dilemma between *Dhārma* and *Kāma* the twin pivots of human existence. It is the only work by Karnad where in the protagonist with his male-consciousness occupies the centre. Thus, it marks a small but definite and important break in the Karnad drama and dramaturgy. In this connection, Jasbir Jain remarks: "Karnad's choice of the priest as the narrative voice, the centrality of the temple as a place for his trial, the worship of the *lingam*—all represent the male principle."[1]

The monologue is based on a folk-tale which belongs to the Chitradurga region of Karnataka. It became widely known, when the Kannada writer T.R. Subbanna includes it in his 1952 novel, *Hamsageethe*. It is a story of Veeranna, a married priest, who falls in the love of a courtesan to whom he takes the offerings from the temple after the everyday prayer. One day, the Chieftain discovers a hair in the *prasad*. In his explanation, Veeranna claims that the hair belongs to God. To prove his explanation, the priest now challenges the God to display hair or accept his head in punishment. He enters a meditative trance for twelve days. On the day of the full moon, the Chieftain arrives. To his surprise, the *Shivalinga* has indeed sprouted long silken hair. The priest's power of worship is confirmed by the miracle of the *Shivalinga*. To check the authenticity, he pulls out a tuft. Blood begins to ooze from the crown of the *lingam*.

Overwhelmed by a sense of sin at having injured his deity and also to save himself from public humiliation, Veeranna beheads himself in the sanctum.

The Play's Theme and Story

The monologue *Flowers* is originally written in English and then translated into Kannada by Karnad himself as "Hoovu". It is first premiered in Bangalore's Ranga Shankara, directed by Royston Abel, with Rajit Kapur playing the role of the protagonist.

Flowers opens in a truly monologue style with the presentation by the priest as indicated here: "I am the priest here. I have lived here all my life.... I spend most of my time with the *linga*..." (243). He had spent his childhood with the *linga*, talking to it, singing to it, even discussing recent political developments with it. He reflected: "This temple, this tank, these rough, grey boulders towering over them, the flowering shrubs and trees, the birds that come and go through the seasons—they are my world, a private universe from which I have never for a moment wanted to step out" (243).

He was a married man and lived along with his wife, two children and his parents in a small place. He used to worship Shiva, the all-encompassing deity of the temple by decorating it beautifully with flowers and that was too with immense care, love, and utmost devotion. Everyday, he tried to invent newer and newer ways to place the garlands over the slippery surface of the *lingam*. The priest's skill was so well known that the Chieftain of the land visited the temple for evening prayers everyday.

However, life underwent a change, when Ranganayaki, a wealthy courtesan visited the temple during one of the *Shivaratri* celebrations. He got mad at the very sight of the blessed mole on her left bosom, nesting just near the cleavage when she bended down to accept the *prasada*. The beautiful shape and the spark in her eyes rendered the priest blind. He felt "I had never lusted for a woman before...." But "During the rest of that week, I started the day impatient for a glimpse of hers" (245).

Powerless in the grip of the carnal desires, the priest went to Ranganayaki. She appreciated his great skill in flower decoration and informed him that she had been longing for her body to be decorated with flowers by him. Night after night, he collected the flowers from the *Shivalinga* before closing the temple and went on to embellish the nude beauty of Ranganayaki. The ritual of decorating her sensuous body and then making love to it became a regular exercise with the priest. Very soon, the surrounding villages came to know of this open secret.

However, the priest's devoted and sincere wife remained calm and quiet. She waited at the doorstep half asleep and half awake, to serve him the dinner, without eating herself. The sense of guilt made the priest remember "I would have a dip in the tank and head home. My wife was awake. She never ate before me. As soon as she heard me splashing in the tank, she would start heating up the food. While I ate, she stood rigid by the door, lanky and impassive, concerned but still. She never once asked me about Ranganayaki. I know she would not" (251).

Time moved like a dream. After waiting for the Chieftain late at night on the day of *tritiya*, the priest ordered his wife to go back home and tiptoed his way Ranganayaki's house with those beautiful flowers collected from *Shivalinga* after performing all the *poojas* at the temple. Obsessed with lust, he "wanted Ranganayaki to go to sleep quietly next to him but she wanted the flowers" (255). The regular duty was performed. However, the tranquillity of the night was shattered by the distant thud. It announced the impending arrival of the Chieftain.

Within a moment, the priest collected back the flowers from the sculpted body of Ranganayaki. By the time the Chieftain reaches the temple, he and his wife had re-decorated *Shivalinga* with over-used flowers. The deity started glowing with the splendid elegance. After the *pooja*, the priest held out the plate of flowers to the solemnly smiling Chieftain. But the smile of the Chieftain vanished, the moment he watched a long hair in the flowers. Everyone in the crowd rightly guessed that it could not be his wife's hair.

An accidental hair in the *prasad* for Chieftain created havoc in the life of the honoured priest, his wife and others. The priest asked the Chieftain to grant him the grace till the full-moon to prove that God "will have long hair" (257). The request was granted. The much awaited full-moon night came soon after. During the twelve days, the priest did not venture out of the temple and had spent his time only in the company of *Shivalinga*.

On full-moon, the Chieftain had come with a group of men and the curious public of the village. The priest opened the doors and all gathered were stunned including the priest to see that God had grown long tufts of hair all over His head. When the hair was inspected, blood oozed out. Considering it the sign of divine wrath, everyone including the Chieftain fell at the feet of the priest requesting him for forgiveness. He was honoured as the state saint.

While serving food, his wife informed him, saying "She is gone." The priest was not ready to shoulder the burden of sainthood. The thought "I had tainted myself" (259) was not allowing him to have the peace of mind. Again, he quarrelled with God and firmly warned Him thus: "God must understand I simply cannot live on His terms" (260). He enters into the water of the tank never to return with a thought that he was "guilty of cruelty to the two women I loved" (260). And then the reflection of the scorpio continues to float upon the pond for a long while.

Critical Interpretation and Appraisal of the Play

Karnad, in this monologue, preserves the central event of the *Shivalinga* sprouting hair but his focus is on the conflict between religious devotion and erotic love. It deals with the triangular relationship: one man in love with two women. The monologue delves deep into the unfathomable depths of human mind and reflects its basic craving for love and sex, which man tries to control for some social as well as individual obligations. The celestial beauty of Ranganayaki, a courtesan, makes the priest fail to control his passion for lust. Karnad's mastery in dealing with the subject of love and sex is clearly noticeable in this play also. The minute details of the relationship of the priest with his two women are worked out very skilfully. The delicacy of the language is in harmony with that of the feelings and passion of the lovers. The wording in the meetings between the priest and the courtesan goes thus: "Ranganayaki stood in the hall, half concealed by a pillar.... She put aside the sari she had wrapped herself in and sat down in front of me.... I had never seen a woman completely naked.... My heart was palpitating so wildly that it threatened to burst my eardrums... Fortunately, Ranganayaki herself was so calm and immobile that any amorous advances were out of question" (248-49). This is the first visit of the priest to Ranganayaki undertaken to decorate her with flowers.

The love relationship is elaborated with utmost care. It is depicted so as to develop quite naturally. The flames of passionate intensity go rising gradually. This happened to both—the priest and Ranganayaki. The priest sheds his initial hesitation and shyness in making love and starts playing the dominating manly role. "This then became the daily routine.... I had to undress her—she would not help me. Sometimes, the knot of her breast-cloth was tied into such a mischievous knot that I threatened to cut it with a knife but she said that was not playing the game, and at other times the cloth fell off without warning at my merest touch, leaving me staring breathlessly at her bare bosom. When I finished decorating her, I would lay down and kiss the mole. With sudden movement, she came alive" (250-51).

In the characterization of the priest's wife, Karnad has portrayed an ideal Indian woman. While making love with the courtesan, the priest remembers: "My wife covered herself with a sari, even when she bathed. On the days I wanted her, I would give her a look she had come to recognise and late at night when everyone was fast asleep, she would crawl up to my room for a furtive scuffle in bed which demanded the minimum of uncovering. There were our two children and my old parents in the house and you never know who might call out for help. The problem, however, was more basic. My wife would have died of shame than be seen naked, even by herself" (248-49). The description also throws light on the restrictions in joint family. She neither complains to him about his extramarital relationship nor does it make any difference to her in performing her duties as a devoted wife. That is why the entry of the courtesan in his life does not affect the priest's love for his wife. He becomes helpless and cannot control himself from visiting Ranganayaki but he returns home with a guilt-conscious mind. He confesses: "But I was distressed at the pain I was causing my wife. I loved her. I knew I had made her a target of vicious gossip" (251). It is this guilt-consciousness towards his wife and Lord Shiva that makes him sacrifice his life. Aparna Dharwadker opines "Karnad... recasts the legend as a conflict between religious devotion and erotic love, undergirded by the priest's guilt at his daily betrayal of his wife. The monologue is a swan song of another kind, a recounting priest's experience as he prepares to drown himself in the temple tank."[2]

The character of the priest's wife symbolizes woman's capacity for endurance. The aspect of sex in this conjugal relationship is also handled with utmost delicacy. On the day of *tritiya*, the priest and his wife are portrayed as waiting for the arrival of the Chieftain. When the formality of *pooja* is over, the priest puts the flower on his wife's palm. He senses that the look in her eyes is inviting him. To control himself, he turns to the *linga*. The hesitation makes him think "Was it because I had lost the habit of making love without bringing flowers into it? The gesture proved fatal. The desire faded, the glow went of her eyes" (254). The place of innate passion is abruptly taken by care and devotion, as she mumbles: "Don't go in the dark. Snakes, poisonous insects. Why don't you stay home?" (254). Towards the end of the monologue, the priest has been honoured as the state saint. When he comes to know that Ranganayaki has left the village, he wonders: "The courtesan was gone and had been replaced by Lord Shiva. I was among the chosen of the Lord and she could not possibly think of herself as a wife now, only as a slave and guardian, all shades of the marital bond expunged in favour of her devotion to me, her good fortune in having me for her husband" (259).

"Dhārma" and "Kāma" here go hand in hand. The priest decorates and worships the *Shivlinga* and the courtesan with equal devotion and intensity. However, the change in the priest's life, that is, the mingling of the spiritual and the carnal remains temporary. But "the miracle of *shivlinga* confirms the power of the priest's worship and marks him as one of the chosen, but it also ends his life."[3] Karnad, once again like that of in his other plays such as *Bali: The Sacrifice,* and *The Fire and the Rain* affirms that true love demands sacrifice.

While writing *Flowers*, Karnad may also have in his mind the character of Praneshacharya in Anantha Murthy's novel *Samskara* since the novel is transformed into a film and he himself has played the role of the priest in 1970. Dharwadker's comment about it goes thus: "Both Praneshacharya and the priest in this monologue sublimate their sexuality into religious fervour, and find sudden release after a lifetime of repression in an illicit union. In both works, renunciation gives way to sensuality, resistance to temptation, purity to pollution. Praneshacharya's liaison with the untouchable prostitute Chandri precipitates a sexual and spiritual crisis that is still unresolved at the end of the novel, though it ends his circumscribed existence in the *agrahara*. Similarly, in *Flowers* the priest's sexual awakening in the home of the courtesan Ranganayaki turns his world of ossified routine upside down, and begins the cycle of falsehood and concealment that culminates in the lie about the *lingam* sprouting hair. He, therefore, enacts Praneshacharya's extended crisis in a highly accelerated form and, by the end of the monologue, is poised on the verge of self-destruction."[4]

The setting of the play involves the temple of Lord Shiva in the lap of nature, the priest's home and that of the courtesan. These two homes stand for two worlds: the world of love and responsibility symbolised by the priest's home and the world of lust and passion symbolized by the courtesan's home. The priest's is a home that needs economic support, denies him privacy and personal life; it is a place where desire is fulfilled secretively. Opposite to it is the home of the courtesan. It is a place "where desire is openly expressed and evoked, where the body is naked and worship and possession go hand in hand.... Love making here is a semi-public act...."[5] If the world of the priest's home offers limited sexual life it is also capable of transcending his mind by the duty provided by his devoted soul, that is, his beloved wife. And if the world of courtesan offers him an open choice to fulfil his sexual passion, it becomes the root-cause of his downfall. So, it is observed that the pitting of these two worlds of piety and passion against each other is the essence of the monologuic play *Flowers*.

The contrast is maintained throughout the monologue. The working places of the priest, that is, the temple and the courtesan's home demand a full concentration and devotion. The act of worship in the case of *Shivlinga* is an elaborate ritual with the bathed priest in wet clothes surrounded by the baskets of flowers and the *aarti thalis*. Since water is considered a purifying element, a dip in the holy tank is a necessary activity. It sets a prelude to the ritual of worship. Contrary to it, in the house of the courtesan, the ritual becomes an act of personal expression and exploration. "Instead of the stone stump there is a living, breathing and sleeping body, vibrant and active. There is no public centrality; instead, it is a private place."[6] In the earlier place, the worshipping with the flowers becomes a sacred activity, while, in the second place, it becomes an act of seduction.

The play explores the priest's distinct sexual relationships: With his wife, it is "a furtive scuffle in bed which demanded the minimum of uncovering" (248-49). But with Ranganayaki, it is totally a different experience: "...the natural smell of her body...,the small of her back,...the gentle mould below her navel,...the firm and tight breasts" (249) and "the mole on her left breast, just near the cleavage" (245) invite the artist in him. The work is same but the objects are different. The beautiful body of Ranganayaki makes him very choosy about the flowers. He states: "Each day, I coxed the flowers to say something special to God and then something entirely different to Ranga" (251).

While pointing out the contrast, Jasbir Jain comments: "Earlier the temple was his shrine, the home only a necessary social structure. Now, the courtesan's house is a daily distraction to be kept apart from both the other places. The courtesan resents the parallel role with the *lingam*.... The sacred and the profane exist as parallels, not as continuities or interactive practices. The narrator's character is no longer integrated or hierarchical, it is heretical, divided and constructed by passion. The man has walked out of the role and has acquired 'subjectivity'; he is a lover and no longer a mere devotee; and desire rather than devotion has taken hold of him."[7]

Side by side, the play also seems to handle covertly, if not overtly, the problem of caste system. Ranganayaki has to worship at the end of others, because she is a courtesan and her presence is considered profane and ill-ominous. The priest narrates it, "The inhabitants of the courtesans' quarters are the last to be admitted, so I knew she was one of them" (245). Similarly, when he returns from Ranganayaki's home, he is "ravenously hungry", "because men can take mistress but cannot eat the food cooked by them".[8] He simply narrates "Ranganayaki had given up teasing me about consuming her body but not the food in her house" (251). While returning from her house, he used to "have a dip in the tank" (251).

Similarly, Karnad is critical of the administrative system which admires flattery from the subordinates. The admiration of Chieftain for flower decorations is followed by his retinues. The priest describes it, thus: "If I have managed to lay out the flowers in a particularly innovative pattern, he nods his head in appreciation, turns to his retinue which, needless to add, obediently spouts various standard phrases in agreement" (244).

Conclusion

The monologue depicts the story of a straightforward man who follows the path of truth. His authenticity is beyond question. He is sincere to life and, therefore, to himself. The guilt in his mind does not allow him to accede to the imposed sainthood—a situation akin to the one in R.K. Narayan's novel, *The Guide*. The whole village venerates him but he is no longer happy. He confesses his guilt—his desecration of sacred space. His mind is not ready to accept any condescension even from

God: "Why has God done this to me? I had only asked Him to give me the courage to live in disgrace, for I knew I had tainted myself.... Why am I worthy of this burden He has placed on my shoulder? I refuse to bear it" (259-60). It is a story of a common man like any of us for whom it is rather difficult to control passion and who wants to live a life only of a common man. That is why he tells: "God must understand, I simply cannot live on His terms" (260). The monologue gives a message: "Religious devotion, like sainthood, does not make a complete man. The transformation from an active devotee to a passive saint, from the male principle symbolising power, control and self-sufficiency to female passivity, surrender and dependence is highly dissatisfying. Through this ending, Karnad chooses to comment upon the demands which religion makes and the closures it enforces."[9]

To sum up, the story of the priest goes beyond time and clime; it is universal. It represents the eternal conflict between spirituality and physicality on symbolic level. The play ends making the audience introspective with a question: Why has the priest sacrificed his life? Jasbir Jain is justified in her claim: "The essence of *Flowers* as presenting the drama of life, lies not merely in its structure or in the temporal-spatial conjunctions but in the compressed narrative of transformation, change, questioning and the complexity of human mind as it fluctuates between desire and power, sacrifice and self-fulfilment in order to hold on to some meaning in life. These features would ensure that Karnad's *Flowers* will not fade but be an effervescent addition to the tradition of Indian theatre."[10]

Notes

1. Jasbir Jain, "*Flowers: A Dramatic Monologue*: Patriarchal Power and the Nature of Sacrifice". *Girish Karnad's Plays: Performance and Critical Perspective*. Ed. Tutun Mukherjee. New Delhi: Pencraft International, 2006, 347.
2. Aparna Dharwadker, "Introduction". *Collected Plays*, Vol. 2. New Delhi: OUP, 2005, xxxii.
3. *Ibid.*
4. *Ibid.*

5. Jasbir Jain, *op. cit.* 347.
6. *Ibid.*, 349.
7. *Ibid.*, 349-50.
8. *Ibid.*, 355.
9. *Ibid.*, 356.
10. *Ibid.*, 357.

NEW PLAYS

11

Broken Images: Ego and Alter-ego

Introduction

Girish Karnad's recent play *Broken Images*, a monologue, appeared in 2005, is remarkable in the sense that it gives a radical turn to his extensive literary career due to the use of modern technology apart from myth, folk-tale, and history. Karnad here explores the contemporary reality to discuss such issues as politics of language, supremacy of literary genre, and the question of identity. It is directed by Karnad himself with K.M. Chaitanya who has handled the stage setting and the technical aspects of the play. The play opens with the lines of the famous poem by T.S. Eliot's *The Waste Land* from which the title of the play is taken:

> ...for you know only,
> A heap of broken images, where the sun beats,
> And the dead tree gives no shelter,... (261)

The very title of the play hints at the theme, that is, the sense of isolation, socio-psychological breakdown in human communication and relationship and overpowering ambition and greed. The setting of the play is remarkable: On one part of the stage, a big plasma television screen is hung which is big enough for a close up view on it and is quite visible for the audience; in the front of it, there is a wide table beside a chair. "The careful design of the setting reinforces the importance of the playwright's optimum exploitation of the play's domain of performance, and not merely its texture and structure, as a means for embodying the theme."[1]

The Play's Theme and Story

The play starts with Manjula Nayak, the protagonist of the play. She seems to be in her mid-thirties/mid-forties. The facial expression reflects her confidence. She is wearing a bright green sari and blouse and a lapel mike. From her remarks, it becomes clear that she is at home, that is, in India and not in London or Toronto in broadcasting studios. While making the mike-testing, she speaks easily and softly over the mike and gets ready for the presentation.

Before Manjula starts making her speech, the announcer appears on the plasma screen against the logo of the TV channel to introduce her: "This evening we broadcast a Kannada telefilm based on this remarkable novel. The film will begin in exactly ten minutes. And we have with us in the studio Ms. Nayak herself, who has graciously agreed to address our viewers about her work. Ladies and gentlemen, welcome the Literary Phenomenon of the Decade, Mrs. Manjula Nayak" (263). As the announcer disappears, Manjula appears on the screen to address the "the invisible audience".

Manjula Nayak is a lecturer in English in Bengaluru. She is known as a Kannada short-story writer till her first English novel *The River has No Memories* surprises the world that wins her the Best Woman Writer of the Year award. The huge advance that she receives from the British publishers brings her name and fame and thereafter makes her resign her job at the college. She is in the studio to talk about her prize-winning book, that is, to deliver a speech to explain the secret of her phenomenal success to her viewers.

In this play, Karnad has used the technique of "a play within a play" which he has already been employed in his early play titled *The Fire and the Rain*. It is a text that incorporates the making of another text. Sitting on the table, Manjula starts speaking. She narrates that, originally, she has been a creative writer in Kannada. She has never attempted to write in English. So, it is her first attempt to write in English. She is conscious of the fact that she will be accused of betraying her mother tongue.

The shift from the regional language to English as the medium of creative writing helps Manjula achieve a large number of readers across the globe. The award seems to justify her shift to England as the medium of Creative Writing. Money, name and fame change her thoroughly. The confidence in her voice and sense of superiority in her appearance and behaviour indicate the resultant effect of the prestigious award. "Interspersing her speech with delicate laughter, she reveals in her new-found status and exhibits, through her voice and gestures, the synonymic variations of 'being superior', that is, to overtrump, outshine, outclass, best...."[2]

The play dwells on certain motifs and deals with some vital issues: (1) the matter of changing surname of a woman on her marriage; (2) the problem of the use of mother tongue and that of English for creative writing; (3) the issue of plagiarism in the realm of creative writing; and (4) the use of novel as the popular genre of creative writing.

Manjula: A New Woman

Karnad's women characters challenge the famous statement made by the veteran feminist Simone de Beauvoir "One is not born but rather becomes a woman..."[3] and the protagonist of the play Manjula is no exception to it.

A woman's identity is related to two homes, that is, her father's home and that of her husband's one. And the decision is often taken by the male-counterpart. Therefore, her identity is always fleeting. At the very beginning of the monologue, the playwright hints at this problem. The protagonist of the play Manjula is a bold, new woman who herself has taken a decision about the use of surname. She states: "Namaskara. I am Manjula Nayak. I must mention that officially I am Mrs. Manjula Murty, but my creative self continues to be Manjula Nayak. There are some areas in which we must not let marriage intrude too much" (263).

Politics of Language

The use of English for creative writing is the hot subject that has held the centre stage of interest not only in India but in all post-colonial countries and cultures even in the middle of the

21st century. While narrating the reactions over the publication of the English novel of Manjula, a mega event in the drama under study, Aparna Dharwadker says: "The switch to English, hailed as an inspired act of self-fashioning on the author's part, turns out in reality to be an act of dishonesty, desperation, and cowardice, the implication being that the material lure of English as a medium can only lead the Indian language author to prostitute herself."[4]

The critics who favour nativism as creed are deadly opposed to the use of English for creative writing. The question that is raised about the first English novel of Manjula is: "After having written in Kannada all your life, why did you choose—suddenly—to write in English? Do you see yourself as a Kannada writer or an English writer? What audience do you write for?" (263).

M.K. Rukhaya, while speaking about the identity crisis in the play, states: "The writer also highlights the age-old conflict between writing in one's own language and a foreign language, through the objective correlative of the writer's confrontation with her own image. Girish Karnad ascertains that the seed of the play was planted in his mind by a conversation that he had with the writer Shashi Deshpande who had an emotional encounter at the writer's conference in Neemrana between the regional writers versus the English writers. Again, on another occasion, the Kannada writer U.R. Ananthamurthy is supposed to have burst out against English writers claiming that English writers were like prostitutes since they wrote with an eye for money and global reach the language offers."[5]

Karnad, through the protagonist of the play Manjula, seems to give reply to these charges levelled against the use of English for creative writing. She is a successful author of short and long fiction in Kannada and a teacher of English in a Bangalore College and has led a rather typical literary life. She unexpectedly publishes a novel in English. The outstanding success of the novel makes her the subject of admiration as well as that of bitter criticism. She is accused of betraying her own language for the sake of name, fame, money, extended audience and publicity stunt. Therefore, "the content of her speech introduces the much debated, complex and the emotionally charged subject of the increasing threat to the regional languages—the mother tongue and, therefore, 'sacred'—and their gradual erasure under the onslaught of English, the language of the alien invaders that had penetrated the 'vernacular' culture."[6]

Pat comes the protagonist's reply: "...if there was a betrayal, it was not a matter of conscious choice. I wrote the novel in English, because it burst out in English. It surprised even me. I couldn't understand why it was all coming out in English. But it did. That's all. There is no other explanation" (264). She further continues: "Recently, the President of the Central Sahitya Akademi—the National Academy of the Letters—... declared that Indians who write in English do so in order to make money...but my response to the charge that I write in English for money would be: Why not? Isn't that a good enough reason? Would you like to see what royalties I earned when I wrote in Kannada?... A Kannada proverb says: "A response is good. But a meaningful response is better." Meaningful: *Arthapoorna*. The Kannada word for Meaning is *Artha*—which also means money! And of course, fame, publicity, glamour...power" (264-65). Karnad, here, straightforwardly seems to express his views on the commercialization of the use of English by the creative writer.

In this connection, Aparna Dharwadker opines: "...Indian-English writers (...such as Nissim Ezekiel, P. Lal, Keki Daruwalla, and Arvind Krishana Mehrotra) claimed that English was not a deliberately chosen or elitist medium, but simply a 'natural' expression of their private and social experience. In the *Broken Images*, the protagonist Manjula Nayak presents the same arguments in defence of her sudden transition...."[7]

Karnad is a playwright who most of the time pens his plays in Kannada first and then translates them into English. *Broken Images* is the first play that was simultaneously staged both in Kannada and English, and therefore, the playwright, here, gives a full stop to the age-old debate over the use of English or that of the mother tongue for creative writing. Dharwadker, very justifiably, remarks: "Karnad's own authorial career, in short, seems to counteract the premise in the *Broken Images* that

English is the necessary bridge to literary and material success for Indian authors, or that English and the Indian languages are mutually exclusive media."[8] In this regard, Manjula appears to be the playwright's mouthpiece, who expresses her views over the debate of the politics of language. Manjula is surprised that the "intellectuals" whom she respects are "writers who were gurus to me, friends who I thought would pat me on my back and share my delight—they are all suddenly breathing fire. How dare I write in English and betray Kannada!" (263). So, she states: "What baffles—actually, let me confess, hurts me—is why our intellectuals can't grasp this simple fact! I have been accused of writing for foreign readers. Accused! As though I had committed a crime. A writer seeks audiences where she or he can find them!" My British publishers said to me: "We like your book, because it's so Indian. We receive any number of manuscripts from Indian but they are all written with the western reader in view. Your novel has the genuine Indian feel!... For Indian writers, English is the medium of dishonesty. Of course, one could also ask how many Kannada writers are honest in what they write—in Kannada" (264).

Plagiarism in Creative Writing

After the language issue, Manjula gets ready to face the queries made about the characters portrayed in the novel, that is, "a person confined to bed all her life". She is asked "How could you so vividly recreate the inner life of a person confined to bed all her life? How can a healthy, outdoor woman be so empathetic to the emotional world of a disabled person?" (265). While replying to the query, Manjula comes out with the statement that she nursed her invalid sister Malini for six years, while the latter lived with her after the death of their parents. Manjula gets very much sensitive and emotional while speaking about her beautiful and gentle sister, who passed away a year ago. She could do nothing but to watch helplessly. The novel centres round the character of Malini. Hers is the only character that is drawn from life; others are entirely fictive. At the end, Manjula acknowledges her husband Pramod for the constant support and encouragement he provides in the process of writing, when she frequently feels floundering, sinking, and utterly clueless. She generously states: "...he was always there at my side encouraging me, prodding me on. Without him, I would never have completed the novel. Thank you Promod" (266).

Manjula has been speaking to the invisible, passive audience, that is, the T.V. viewers. She finished her talk in the stipulated time and concludes by saying "Well, that is it. I have committed the cardinal sin of writing in English" (laughs) (266). She gets relieved and is about to leave the studio. However, her image on the plasma screen of the television suddenly becomes alive and it starts speaking to her.

In the course of conversation, gradually and painfully, various aspects of Manjula's life and nature are exposed, including her relationship with her husband and also that with her sister.

Malini, Manjula's sister, occupies the centre of the plot of the novel. She suffered from meningomyelocele, a disease in which a person is disabled for life due to dysfunction of the nervous system. Manjula was rather envious of her sister who was intelligent, lively, even though she was confined to the wheel-chair. She was "the apple of her parents' eye" (269) and was always the focus of attention. Manjula had to settle for second place and was constantly disregarded. Malini excelled in all areas over Manjula—in looks and in intelligence. Manjula was made to stay with her grandparents who loved her, but who were, according to her, "no substitute" (269) for parents. The most cherished moments of her life were the times she spent with her parents during her vacations. It was later that she met Pramod, married him and settled down in Jayanagar. Her father left most of his assets in Malini's name. After her parents' death, Manjula shoulders Malini's responsibility.

The speech brings to surface Manjula's resentment for living quite away from parents, her envy and anger for her sister's delicate looks and for the easy companionship she shared with her husband Pramod. Pramod, being a software engineer, worked from home most of the time, and finally found his intellectual match in Malini. Pramod strove to discover new ways of entertaining himself. Manjula doubts that Pramod fantasized and romanticized more about Malini than herself. However, she confesses: "I was not as bright and studied painstakingly. I often wondered whether I would have been so bright if I'd received all that love and affection" (269). She tried her hand at creative writing too but could write only in Kannada, Manjula states: Malini "...breathed, laughed, dreamt in English. Her friends spoke only in English. Having her in my house for six years helped improving my English" (271).

While speaking about Manjula's and Malini's personal lives, Tutun Mukherjee states: "The relentless inquisition continues. More 'truths' are revealed, more 'facts' are acknowledged. The Image operates as a psychological *camera obscura* into Manjula's soul.... Manjula's explanations continue, peeling away the layers of duplicity, deception and falsehood and exposing her discontentment, her secret yearnings for attention, the repressed covetousness for what was beyond her reach."[9]

Finally, Manjula, through the exchange of dialogues, admits, though agitatedly, that she has committed a guilt:

> Manjula: All right! I didn't write the novel. She did. She wrote it. Every word of it. ...after her death, I found the typescript in her drawer. I read it. (Pause) I was decimated. (282)
>
> Image: It was brilliant. A masterpiece.... The work of a genius. You knew that as a writer you could never dream of such heights. The passion. The clarity. The insights. The total control. A work of genius. (283)

The protagonist in the novel describes Manjula as "the first cousin, and not sister...a shallow woman, a pretentious mediocrity...and devious relative who had taken her in for her inheritance" (284-85). That is the image of Manjula for her sister and husband. However, Manjula accepts: "But there were no adjectives. Just facts. The events were from life. They were accurately described.... I couldn't deny them.... I hated the cripple. I had always hated her. I was only waiting for her to die" (285).

Malini's mistake in putting her name as M. Nayak gives Manjula a golden opportunity to grab what she could never think of or even dream of to achieve. Taking M. as Manjula she successfully manages to take the credit of writing the novel as well as to steal Malini's identity. This brings out the latent hatred she possesses for Malini all through her life. She achieves victory over her crippled, genius, younger sister but that is, posthumously, of course.

But the Image on the screen does not allow her to enjoy herself with that moment also by making her conscious of the fact: "...everyone would see who 'the first cousin' was. You would become the laughing stock. Worse still.... Malini had nicely crucified you" (285).

The character of the Image is a dramatic device through which Manjula's conscience and morality are exposed towards the end of the play. Aparna Dharwadker in her characteristic remarks puts forth the central idea of the play: "Manjula's conversation with her own television image (her doppelganger) soon reveals, however, that she is an imposter who has passed off her dead sister Malini's novel as her own. The switch to English, hailed as an inspired act of self-fashioning on the author's part,... Significantly, the value of the novel itself is not in dispute—titled *The River has No Memories*, it is a superbly accomplished autobiographical fiction about a lifelong invalid who 'breathed, laughed, dreamt in English'. What the play impugns is the opportunism of the Kannada author who tries to cash in on a dead sibling's talent."[10]

Side by side, Karnad also highlights the issue of supremacy that exists in literary genre, particularly, in the context of contemporary Indian literature and comes out with a conclusion that "...a play in English, however successful its author, cannot compete with a novel in English because of the qualitative differences between novels and plays as literary artifacts. Fiction in English by Indian and Indian diaspora authors now commands a global readership and appears in academic curricula around the world; Indian plays in English occupy a distinctly subservient position...."[11]

Conclusion

So, to sum up, we see the simulated image on the screen hinting at Manjula's inner voice, her conscience, her alter-ego that gives her a feel of guilt and crushes her pride ruthlessly. The dramatist seems to convey that "play begins with a false image of Manjula giving her speech on the achievement before the television camera but ends with her confrontation with reality, that is the voice of her inner self or moral conscience."

The play, thus, dwells on the problem of the woman's identity, her shrewd, crafty nature, her over-ambitiousness and selfish design in the pursuit of her career and, further, marks the protagonist's journey towards "broken images" and "dead trees" offering no shelter.

Notes

1. Tutun Mukherjee, "The Splintered Self: *A Heap of Broken Images* at Rangshankara". *Girish Karnad's Plays: Performance and Critical Perspective*. Ed. Tutun Mukherjee. New Delhi: Pencraft International, 2006, 334.
2. *Ibid.*, 336.
3. Simone de Beauvoir, "Part IV: The Formative Years". *The Second Sex*. New York: Vintage, 1989, 267.
4. Aparna Dharwadker, "Introduction". *Collected Plays*. Vol. 2. New Delhi: OUP, 2005, xxvii.
5. M.K. Rukhaya, "Identity Crisis in Girish Karnad's *A Heap of Broken Images*". http://www.the-criterion.comV1n1April2010. *The Criterion: An International Journal in English.*
6. Tutun Mukherjee, *op. cit.*, 336.
7. Aparna Dharwadker, "Introduction". *op. cit.*, xxviii.
8. *Ibid.*, xxx.
9. Tutun Mukherjee, *op. cit.*, 340-41.
10. Aparna Dharwadker, "Introduction". *op. cit.*, xxvii.
11. *Ibid.*, xxx.

12

Wedding Album: Exploring Indian Culture

Introduction

Wedding Album (2009) is the most recent play of Girish Karnad. It is the translation of his Kannada play *Maduveya Album* (2006). The play gives the picture of a typical Indian arranged marriage. Away from myths, folktales and history, the dramatist here deals with the contemporary Indian society with a view to exhuming the reality of Indian culture and the politics of the tele-serials and Internet cafés, used as a means for the fulfilment of erotic fantasies. The play also throws light on a traditional Indian wedding and, through it, explores the strained relations which get exposed on the occasion of a wedding. Karnad, here, harshly denigrates the Indian cultural norms, purity of familial relationships, and the general tendency of the expatriate Indians to expect serenity and sincerity from their Indian housewives. According to Amrit Srinivasan,

> *Wedding Album* works as (a) modern myth, whose condensed logic straddles both the real and the tech-simulated world of today, to help us confront our own mixed-up, amoral, craven, unhappy selves ... Karnad, thus, reverses the charge laid against him sometimes that his pre-occupation with history and folk myth makes him evade contemporary Indian reality.[1]

The play starts with the preparation of Vidula's wedding, a girl from Saraswat Brahmin family and the female protagonist of the play, with Ashwin, the stereotype of the American NRI. Both of them know each other only through electronic media such as e-mails, video-conferencing and photo-sharing. The marriage of Vidula and Ashwin represents the synthesis of tradition and modernity, since it appears as an arranged marriage with the cooperation of post-modern technologies by a conservative social institution. The play projects the contemporary Indian society, which is changing rapidly under the impact of several global forces. Through the character of Ashwin, the dramatist portrays the problems of the non-resident Indians in search of their cultural roots.

The Play's Theme and Story

The play *Wedding Album* starts with a flashback technique. Scenes One and Five take place about three years after the rest of the play. It is structured into nine scenes. It depicts a normal urban, educated, liberal middle-class family: Actually, it is the album of the Nadkarni family having two daughters and a son, elder daughter, Hema, who lives in Australia with her professional husband, son Rohit who is a software designer, writes stories and scripts for tele-plays, and a younger daughter Vidula who is happy enough to marry a suitable boy from the US she has never met. The playwright also deftly portrays the characters of father, mother and the cook Radhabai.

Scene One of the play takes place in a Software Production Office with Pratibha Khan (40), and Rohit (32). Vidula is exhibited on the screen in close-up, speaking directly to the camera. She is trying to introduce herself and her family to Ashwin Panje, an expatriate Hindu in America. Actually, Rohit is narrating a story for a tele-serial to Pratibha. He says: "Pratibhaji, it actually happened. Just three years ago.... She hasn't come home in the three years since her marriage.... She becomes pregnant. Miscarried. He was worried about her frail health, so wouldn't send her home. She is expecting again" (8-9).

From Scene Second, the play starts with the mood of the celebration of the wedding of Vidula to the video groom, Ashwin. Although in America, Ashwin has a mixed feeling for this country. For him, America is both the land of opportunity and the NRI's burden.

> ...it is shallow..., glittering and shallow. The European Industrial Revolution began by rejecting religion in favour of material values. But today this legacy is strangling the west. They have no spiritual moorings left. They are adrift in godless, amoral world.... Unlike the US, India has an ancient civilization. A culture which is full of wisdom and insight. India should have the capacity to lead the world. (80-81)

Karnad also introduces the other members of the Nadkarni family on the occasion of wedding preparations. This occasion displays the mutual concern, as well as the anxieties and resentments long buried within the bosom of the family. The older generation—father and mother consider themselves outdated and therefore, useless in the new technological turmoil. "A wedding" for Mr. Nadkarni, "is essentially an excuse for shopping" (31) and for Mrs. Nadkarni, Vidula's mother, "A wedding means expenses—there is no getting away from that" (15). The family members are portrayed through their reactions to Vidula's marriage.

The members of the young generation—brother Rohit and elder sister Hema—possess aspirations to easy prosperity. Hema appears a rational and progressive mother. Rohit symbolises the self-centred and hypocritical modern youth who is ready to sacrifice human values for his selfish motive, viz. the better career prospects.

Through Rohit, the play displays how the craze for money and fame could make a person opportunistic. Rohit loves Isabel, but he does not want to marry her. The Sirur family successfully prevails on him to marry their daughter Tapasya. They offer him foreign education and even assistance in setting up his own business. Rohit, at first, strongly refuses but gradually gets ready and leaves Isabel to suffer. Rohit seems to be the spokesman of the careerist youth of this so-called cultured Indian society who uses friendship as well as matrimonial relationship in keeping with the necessity of time. Rohit marries Tapasya and yet has an eye on Isabel. So, he invites her to join him when Tapasya is with her parents for her delivery.

Tapasya, Rohit's wife is a peripheral character. She is the daughter of Gopal and Vatsala Sirur from Hyderabad. Her only brother Sharad is in America and her parents think that all their property will go to their daughter; hence, they propose Rohit alluring that they can even sponsor his trip abroad. Mira Hattangadi from Hubli is Gopal Sirur's sister and a distant relative of the Nadkarnis. The couple works as the mediator between the Nadkarnis and the Sirurs to arrange the marriage between Rohit and Tapasya. The Third Scene of the play, thus, presents the persuasion of Rohit by the Sirur and Hattangadi families and all their rubbish bargains and hazels to marry their daughter to him even though Rohit is utterly unwilling to entertain them.

Hema is the elder daughter of the Nadkarni family. She comes to Dharwad for her sister's proposed marriage. This mature lady in appearance bears a grudge against her parents for not spending as much money on her wedding 15 years back as that on Vidula's one. Whatever is offered in Vidula's wedding to her and to her husband, she rejects quite unhappily. In the Seventh Scene, father's remarks throw light on it. He says: "This time she's really overdoing it. I am tired of her nagging us about how we spent nothing on her wedding" (73).

Vivan Kaikini, the 13-year-old boy of neighbourhood, is the representative of those adolescent boys in the society who possess lust for the grown-up women. He is obsessed by Hema who happens to be his mother's age and goes on writing notes expressing his wild fantasies for her. Surprisingly enough, Hema, too, finds it soothing her senses towards the end of the play. But when Vivan's friend Ambuja comes to Dharwad, he gives up his wild sentiments for Hema by telling Radhabai to convey to Hema "I can't come tomorrow. Or ever again" (92).

Ramdas' story also indicates the exploitation of women within the family. Ramdas Nadkarni hankers after his sister-in-law, that is, mother of Vidula, Rohit, and Hema. Throughout the play, the father, is shown remembering Ramdas, his younger brother who is no longer staying with the family. The play exposes his unexpressed sentiments when Vidula tries to get her birth-certificate as a necessary document for her visa to America. On the birth-certificate, Ramdas uncle had put his own name instead of her real father's. But mother's reaction to it also reveals the dual aspect of her personality. In the beginning, she expresses great deal of anger and disappointment at this mistake but later on, she suggests let it be as it is instead of a change. Hema, too, remembers how her uncle used to protect her mother, against the wrath of her father. Ramdas' anger for his brother for behaving cruelly with his wife indirectly throws light on the longing he possesses for his sister-in-law. Thus, the play delineates the degeneration of the joint-family system in the 21st century.

The sub-plot of the play deals with the life-story of Radhabai who is serving as a cook in the Nadkarni family for seven long years. The tragic incidents in her life bring some vital changes in her otherwise calm and quiet nature. It is through the conversation between Vidula and Hema that the life-story of Radhabai is revealed.

Radhabai was a poor woman from a village. Yamuna, her daughter goes to Bengaluru in search of a job. After getting it, she used to send money to her parents in village. After her husband's death, Radhabai, too, goes to Bengaluru and finds a job as a cook with a family in Malleswaram. Life in Bengaluru reveals to her the tragic reality that her daughter has turned a concubine maintained by a rich trader. Radhabai keeps this fact a secret since she is scared about losing her job at the mention of her daughter. Due to the gap of communication between the two, Radhabai goes to meet Yamuna but only to know that the trader had suddenly died and Yamuna had been thrown out by his family; so, she's gone, leaving no trace for her mother. With no shelter or money and heaps of insults from people, she goes mad and starts running on streets in search of her mother. Surprisingly enough, Radhabai refuses to recognise her when she finally finds her house.

The incident, however, leaves Radhabai guilty and repentant, causing her to weigh and ponder her decision time and again, throwing her into fits of temper. The play ends with Radhabai contemplating the decisions she made, reliving the crucial moments and justifying to herself what she did and why she could not do otherwise. It appears that she repeats the incident to herself time and again in order to consider and reconsider her options: "You can't keep a grown up daughter at home, can you? (92). ...I was paralyzed. Why is she here? What if my mistress sees her? What'll happen to me?"[2] (93).

The tragic incident has a deep impact on Radhabai's mind. It renders her angry and frustrated. The drastic change in Radhabai's behaviour is noticed by the family members. In the course of time, they come to know of the tragedy. Vidula informs Hema how once Radhabai suddenly got agitated while watching the TV, when they present a mother sacrificing her life to save her daughter. This otherwise usual story disturbs Radhabai a lot, for she takes it as a sort of an offence due to her guilt-ridden consciousness.

Although Radhabai's story is used as a sub-plot in the play, yet it certainly catches the eye of Pratibha Khan when she is listening to the themes by Rohit for the next episodes of their TV serial. Rohit is showing the tape to Pratibha Khan prepared for Vidula's marriage to Ashwin. Later on, he also narrates Radhabai's tragic story to her. Pratibha finds it more realistic and melodramatic than Vidula's episode. They discuss how they can mould the ending of Radhabai-Yamuna story a little to make it even more tragic and touching. Pratibha congratulates Rohit for having thought of such a great idea, "...your great advantage is that you know the lower middle class inside out" (59). The manipulation of real life tales to suit the requirements of a tele-serial suggests how far sensibilities can be shaped by media as a part of publicity stunt. People do not hesitate in the least in utilizing human grief as a marketable commodity.

Vidula's story has no appeal to Pratibha. She remarks: "They (audience) may believe it, but they won't like it. A girl from an educated middle-class family—a graduate—agrees to consider marrying a man whom she has never met. The boy turns up, all ready to jump on the altar without ever having seen her. In this day and age" (8).

Vidula is an educated modern girl; hence, why she agrees to such an arrangement is left incomprehensible. However, when the preparation of the wedding is going on, she represents herself as another lady in the Internet café. Her conversation with her unknown friend reveals the dark aspect of her personality. Yamuna's tragic life has a great impact on Vidula's mind, too. Considering herself in the place of Yamuna, she starts talking with Swami Ananga Nath through Internet. Thus, she steps into the shoes of another girl, as the concubine of an older man who treats her like a slave. The girl is sold off when the master dies. But whatever she reveals to this unknown friend at the other end is only the invention of her imagination. The Internet conversation offers her a veil of secrecy behind which she can be whatever she feels like. This multiple performance on the part of Vidula brings into focus her unfulfilled, suppressed desires which she tries to fulfil anonymously with the help of the modern technology. "Karnad this time takes his reader/audience on an uncensored tour of contemporary India thereby demystifying and deconstructing two vital institutions in India called marriage and family."[3]

The character of Vidula is the example of a split-personality. She willingly steps into a newly constructed 'self' in the Internet café. At the same time she accepts to perform the role of Ashwin's bride-groom. This strain of hypocrisy in Vidula's personality is noticed in the Opening Scene of the play. Her brother Rohit is making a video of Vidula to be sent to Ashwin. When he asks her to appear bright and cheerful, she abruptly objects to him, saying "I just want him to know what I am like"; and she warns Ashwin, "I am not glamorous, as you can see. I am not exceptional in any way. I don't want you to be disappointed later" (6).

Vidula pretends to be timid and subservient. However, the scene in the Internet café unveils her hypocrisy. When she is attacked by the self-styled guardians of the Hindu culture, she reacts in an aggressive and rude manner, using expletives and threatening them that she will inform the matter to the police that they have attempted to rape her: "What gives you the right to come in here. I'll do what I like here. Who the hell are you to question me?... You have come here to rape me, haven't you?" (70). And later, "Get out of here, you bloody bull-shitters..." (71). Vidula transforms into a bold, aggressive woman who is alert enough of her rights and has the guts to fight against the patriarchal norms which let men free to commit adultery and tries to impose the norms of purity of the so-called cultured society only on women. She has the capacity to protect her individuality. Similarly, her conversation with the bodyless brings forth the thirst for lust in the mind of the girls in the conservative, orthodox families.

Autobiographical Elements in the Play

According to Girish Karnad's authentic statement, this play has taken 30 to 40 years in its making. When his sister got married, he watched the members of his family gathering together and observed the resultant, interpersonal dynamics and tensions...he found it a combination of 'celebration and anxiety' and tucked it away in the mind, to emerge much later. He didn't want to write it as a 'story' play though,...the form that it has taken now is satisfying to him[4] (Citizen Matters.in).

Karuna Patange states: "One could easily trace the origin of various characters and incidents of the play in the dramatist's life: while reading the memoirs of his life *Aadaadta Aayushya* one becomes aware of this, e.g. the father in the play is like Karnad's own father—a retired doctor, who (has) never entered a private practice and, hence, (has) never owned a house of his own; the elder daughter Hema of the play, like Karnad's own elder sister is settled abroad after marriage; also there are references to her childhood, spent away from her parents due to father's constant transfers. The mother and father of *Wedding Album* express this guilt a few times while talking about Hema; the curious episode of the play in which it is revealed that Vidula's birth certificate bears her uncle Ramdas' name in place of the father's too has autobiographical reference."[5]

Critical Interpretation and Appraisal of the Play

In *Wedding Album*, Karnad deals with the cultural degradation and thereby exposes the Hindu fundamentalism that claims for purity of race and culture in the Indian context. He very candidly scrutinizes the hidden passions, lurking sexual desires that deep-rooted beneath apparent layers of cultural sophistication. The play is a scathing criticism on the Hindu rituals and institutions called marriage and family that are considered to be the holiest of holy in the Indian set-up. Amrit Srinivasan very justifiably states:

> The constellation of sexual, conjugal, caste, class, and age-related behaviours and attitudes of selfishness and sacrifice, chastity and commerce, obedience and authority, all integral to modern Hindu marriage, forms *Wedding Album*'s central narrative thread.[6]

The proposed marriage between an Indian middle class Saraswat Brahmin girl in Dharwad and the NRI brings to surface the duality of human psyche. An expatriate American young man is fed up with the West. He tries to find spiritual satisfaction and stability by marrying a girl from Dharwad. However, he is quite ignorant of the fact that this apparently simple, shy, meek, tender-looking girl fulfils her erotic fantasies by visiting the darkness of the Internet café. His denunciation of the Western culture as devoid of values and choosing of the Eastern one considering it to be pure one proves faulty. The events and incidents in the life of family members of Nadkarni indicate that Indian culture and traditions quite ironically have no longer been remained that serene, great, and glorious. Karnad, in this play, nullifies the very concept of purity of Indian culture.

The play also focuses on the naked reality of the Indian society, which remained patriarchal yet in the 21st century where women are taken for granted by their male-counterparts. Vidula's arranged marriage with Ashwin is in a way similar to the master-slave arrangement of Vidula's imagination. Karnad obliquely hints at the patriarchal ownership of a woman at her father's as well as at her husband's home. Vidula informs: "He is dying. He has had a heart attack. Last night. He is in the ICU. Could be dead by tomorrow. His family is bound to throw me out. So, I had to find a new master. A younger man. He lives in the US. He has paid a good price to my family" (64).

Her sister Hema, too, discusses the patriarchal arrangement in her married life, where her husband takes all the decisions:

"Because they are all transferable jobs and the white wife refuses to go trailing after her husband. We Indian women, on the other hand, are obedient Sati Savitris, ever willing to follow in our husband's footsteps. Look at me.... Our men may get all the top jobs. But I am in no better position than Ma" (17). It is for this reason that Hema has not been able to utilise her talent and education and remains a housewife, constantly worrying about her children and home.

The indifference of her husband and father may be the cause that makes Hema feel soothing for the attraction of the adolescent boy Vivan towards her. However, towards the end of the play, Vivan gives up this romantic relationship for a younger girl. Karnad, through this episode, hints at the sexual openness prevalent in the so-called cultured Indian society where all limitations of age, relation and propriety disappear. Similarly, Hema's remark about her father-in-law brings to notice how the lust for passion in mind makes man blind. She says: "...during our (my) wedding, I caught my father-in-law looking at me" (51).

The character of Nagappa shows the exploitation of small girls even by the household servants. When mother praises Nagappa, the previous cook in the family, Vidula states: "True, Nagappa didn't raise his voice. But a lot of his energy went into raising skirts." Hema gets shocked and says: "But you were so little. I never thought—". To this Vidula's retorts saying: "He would touch one in the oddest spots" (23).

Ashwin, apparently appears straightforward, but the playwright obliquely disseminates the patriarchal traits in his personality. Ashwin's high-sounding words about preservation and propagation of Hinduism and Indian culture, too, appear to be a professional tactic to win people's minds and impress them. After enjoying himself with the free life in America, he decides to marry an Indian girl from Dharwad and expects from her honesty and sincerity. He imagines the girl would be steeped in "innocence" and "purity" (81). He confesses to Vidula: "I have drunk life in the US to the lees. Girl friends, affairs, mistresses, one-night stands and on the public stage, glamour, success, social connections. I have been through them all. And I have come to the conclusion that whole culture is empty of values now, bereft of any living meaning" (80).

Ashwin is the best example of those people who try to exploit the life-partners by making them stereotyping gender in the name of discourses of religion and culture. He expects Vidula to be a submissive housewife, who should perform her duties within the circle of the household without expecting any gratitude or without thinking of her own life, career or economic independence. Ashwin tactically yet spontaneously uses the patriarchal discourse of woman as Devi. He tells Vidula, "Someone like you carries within you the essence of Hindu spirituality. Woman as mother, wife, daughter. Womanhood as the most sacred ideal" (81).

Vidula, however, listens to Ashwin in silence and does not object to it. This situation, too, is ironic, since the audience/reader who has witnessed Vidula's reality in the Internet café in Scene Six know that Ashwin is vainly trying to seek cultural purity, innocence and all the glorified images of women in Vidula. It is difficult to believe that she is the same Vidula who reprimanded the moral guardians in the café episode so strongly. In this connection, Amrit Srinivasan opines:

> Never mind that Vidula is not exactly as he (Ashwin) pictures her and that like any other modern, mixed up, unhappy, Hindu gal ('timid' is how her mother sees her), she leads a secret life. Whether willingly submitting herself as Kuchla the Jezebel to the disembodied randy voice of Swami Ananga Nath the Bodyless, in a darkened Cyber Café, or transmuting her guilt at being found out into hysterical rage, screaming 'sexual harassment' to make her moral tormentors run away—she is resourceful enough to find herself a surrogate swami, a flesh and blood stranger to help her work her way through hopeless desire. The subjugation she seeks in her secret, erotic world can after all be served as well through man and marriage and to higher purpose.[7]

The character of mother seems to have emerged, untouched from the influence of patriarchy. She is subjected to severe beatings from her husband. But, now, it is she who takes the decisions. Father praises Ma for her sacrifice and her skill at management. But this, again, reinforces the idea that a woman can only win appreciation in a patriarchal system, if she makes sacrifices, reaffirming the woman as *Devi*. While pointing out the change in the character of mother Amrit Srinivasan remarks:

> The traditional wife, it is true, sequestered herself aggressively and possessively in this very private space, a willing mistress/slave of the culinary realm.... But for Mrs. Nadkarni, Vidula's mother, the kitchen has become a parody—a battleground for class supremacy and control over Radhabai, the willing but competing female shadow in the kitchen, with whom she boxes away to no conclusion whatsoever, to relieve herself of her sense of failure and unfulfilment vis-à-vis the family.[8]

Rohit's decision to marry Tapasya confirms the burning reality in Indian society that marriage is used as a means of achieving the goal or target. Rohit's relationship with Isabel cannot materialize into a marriage apparently due to Isabel's jealousy and misunderstanding, and Rohit's opportunistic nature. For him, career is more important than love. Naturally, he takes material advantages of marrying a girl of his own caste belonging to a wealthy family who undertakes the responsibility to bear the expenses of his trip abroad for training.

Karnad pooh-poohs the ridiculous conventions in the Indian society pertaining to marriage from *muhurat* to bribing the suitable boy by offering him the girl's property. The institution called marriage in India is rudely exposed and highly satirized in the play. Tapasya, though silent, indicates the devaluation of women in the entire process of an arranged marriage. Here, she is just a puppet controlled by her parents' will and the most suitable boy's choice.

Vidula is at the pivot of the main plot. She mentions herself having been sold off in Scene Six during her erotic conversation with the voice of Swami Ananga Nath, the Bodyless. It's quite significant and highly ironic that she had introduced herself as a, "...kept women. Kept by a trader. I am his concubine. Maintained by a man much older than me" (64). This is Vidula presenting herself as Kuchla, the Jezebel, and a fake character that is based upon another real character Yamuna, reversing the end however. Yamuna has to disappear, lost in the crowd, shunned by her mother, whereas this one Vidula gets a new buyer as revealed through her dialogues in the dark room.

However, the last scene of the play presents "Vidula going abroad to live with Ashwin with a firm determination to be his faithful life-partner forever. She denies Hema's and Rohit's suggestions to divorce Ashwin...if things don't work out" (86). Very calmly, she assures her siblings, "I'll never divorce Ashwin.... Ashwin may not speak much. But he was clear about what he expected from marriage. I agreed with him. I gave him my word.... I have given up eating fish.... I trust him. He is my husband after all" (86-87).

While presenting the burning issues of the contemporary society, Karnad "takes the risk of locating *Wedding Album* in a dreadfully familiar space—the Nadkarni's living room. Given that the story is about a wedding, the bedroom is conspicuously absent...the kitchen, the courtyard, and the inner sleeping quarters remain present in the wings all through the play, except when replaced by the corporate, commercial space of the television production studio, the Internet café, and the restaurant. The birth registration, passport and visa office, the city street, market, and airport, and the expat Hindu homes in Australia and the USA remain vibrant spaces, connected to all or some of the sites of action through phones, computer, car, plane, auto-rickshaw, and mobile communication."[9]

Karnad's plays represent the bold new women in the society who try to establish their identity and individuality and *Wedding Album* is no exception to it. In the portrayal of his characters, Karnad maintained a total objectivity. The women characters in this play have created their own universe. They think and argue and have the voice of protest. They are bold enough to challenge the norms of the society and to follow the dictates of their hearts. However, women's emotional pains and sufferings and her self-endurance are voiced at different points in the play.[10]

In majority of his earlier plays, Karnad has used myth to reflect the contemporary reality. In this play, the old myth is replaced by a new myth, that of the modern technology. This world of sophisticated technology, particularly, encourages a girl from traditional middle class family to bring out her erotic, subconscious which can be interpreted as the representative of techno-savvy young generation.

By making 'distance' technology almost a character in the play, Karnad is able to demonstrate its constant co-operation in the contemporary South Indian Brahmin home, street and office, which underwrites the transnational embeddedness of their lives.[11]

Conclusion

Girish Karnad here exhumes the contemporary Indian society and thereby represents the naked reality lies underneath this sophisticated surface. Such a direct confrontation with dark lives of the younger generation is more than a shock to the conservative mind. The play is a ruthless dissection of the Indian culture which is assumed to be pure and serene. It discusses such issues as the plight of women in a patriarchal set-up, rising middle class Hindu fundamentalism, degeneration of once rich cultural values, the techno-crazy generation and their futile obsessive fantasies and obsessions.[12]

Vidula, the protagonist, represents a woman of the 21st century at the whirlwind of convention and modernity. The play is a brilliant blend of the use of tradition and technology in order to create a strong indictment of the contemporary society. The Internet café is used as a mirror that holds a true picture of the current social order. It brings to notice the wrong use of technology by the young generation. The physical absence of the persons in the Internet café makes them express their suppressed feelings and unfulfilled desires quite openly. It is an open-ended play that makes the audience introspective to think about the direction the young generation is going in—their goal and destination.

Notes

1. Amrit Srinivasan, "Foreword". *Wedding Album*. Girish Karnad. New Delhi: OUP, 2009, ix.
2. From Myth, Folklore and History to Modernity: Subjectivity as a Locus of Conflicts in Girish Karnad. Chapter Three. p. 172. http://shodhganga.inflibnet.ac.in/bitstream/10603/2092/9/09_chapter%203pdf-Internet Explorer
3. Karuna P. Deshmukh, "*Wedding Album*: A Study in its Portrayal of Contemporary Reality", Vol. III, Issue I, April 2014 Impact Factor 0.612. www.ycjournal.net Received: 04 /04/14 Reviewed: 06/04/14 Accepted: 08 /04/14, 191.
4. Quoted in N. Velmani."From Myth to Modernity: A Critical Study of Girish Karnad's *Wedding Album*". *Language in India*. www.languageinindia.com, 13:6 June 2013.
5. Karuna P. Deshmukh, *op. cit.*, 191.
6. Amrit Srinivasan, *op. cit.*, viii-ix.
7. *Ibid.*, xi.
8. *Ibid.*, xvi.
9. *Ibid.*, x-xi.
10. *Ibid.*, xv.
11. *Ibid.*, xi.
12. Karuna P. Deshmukh, *op. cit.*, 193.

13

Boiled Beans on Toast: Aspiration and Frustration

Introduction

> A lonely housewife regains her lost singing voice in a hospice; for a small-town job-seeker the concrete jungle rolling over the shrinking greenery holds promise of untold prospects; for the conservative old lady from the country the race course opens up visions of power; a village woman with an ambiguous past struggles to find a foothold amidst the urban chaos.[1]

This is what Karnad's latest play *Boiled Beans on Toast* communicates. The play has a mythological origin. It is related to the myth in the eleventh century attached to the name of the city as Bengaluru or Bangalore. According to the ancient lore, the King Veera Ballala II of the Hoysala Empire lost his way when he was out for hunting in the forest. After much wandering throughout the night, hungry and thirsty, he came across a lonely hut. It was a dwelling of an old woman who fed him a handful of *benda kalu*, that is, boiled beans and saved his life. With a great sense of gratitude, the king named the spot *Bendakaluru* (the place of boiled beans). In the course of time, Bendakaluru gets corrupted as 'Bengaluru'. Bangalore is the anglicized term given by the colonial rulers to 'Bengaluru', and toast is a British term accepted by the Indians. The Kannada title of the play is *Benda Kaalu on Toast*.

Bengaluru is known for its massive cosmopolitan populace, its progress in IT, pleasant weather, cheap beer and deadly traffic. However, very little has been written or seen or heard about its average resident, that is, housewives, the non-IT professionals, labourers, senior citizens, and others. This latest play by Karnad revolves round the unsung tales of ordinary Bengaluru citizens and their struggles. No doubt, the play's title is linked with a myth but the play marks a total departure from Karnad's famous plays steeped in historical and mythological themes.

The play is directed by Lilette Dubey. It has its premiere show at the NCPA. The curious set consists of Kannada film posters, a popular coffee shop sign board, some chic Fab India type home furniture and some other set pieces. It provides a symbolic backdrop of the rarely visited side of the city of Bengaluru. The same set is the cover-page of the book published by the OUP, New Delhi. This interesting, bulky and oddly angled set appears to be a foregrounding device that attracts the attention of the audience/readers and render them spell bound and disturbed.

The play is translated into Marathi by Pradeep Viddya as *Uney Pure Shahar Ek* (*One City, More or Less*) and has its premiere in February 2013 under the direction of Mohit Takalkar. The locale is transposed from Bengaluru to Pune. The transposition was fit and perfect. "...Pune has followed a graph of growth to Bangalore's progressing from an old, leafy university town to an overcrowded city dominated by information technology and the service industry."[2]

The Play's Theme and the Story

Speaking about the theme of the play, Priya Adarkar opines: "Bengaluru is said to have acquired its name through a king's gratitude for a dish of boiled beans. Bengaluru on toast—a place that has been cooked rapidly from (the) traditional to (the) modern, from a small town into a large metropolis, is the theme of the play: it is the portrait of the city."[3]

The play begins in a different manner. As the lights come on, all the characters are shown immobile, frozen in the middle of some activity. When the lights are fully on, the immobile characters all of a sudden spring into action. A type of chaotic atmosphere is exhibited through the actors talking, moving about, fighting, shouting, and bumping into each other. The background noise of traffic and music adds to the effect of a busy thoroughfare in Bengaluru. Then, the lights and music fade out together. The very first scene sets the theme of the play.

The play starts in the neat living room of the Padabidri family, with the minor characters such as Vimala, Muttu, the maid servants of the Padabidri family and Muttu's mother and brother Shankar. The main action takes place in the scene three where the sophisticated forty—something Anjana Padabidri sits chatting with her pretentious friend Dolly as Vimala and Muttu run in and out of the room getting the household chores done and tea and snacks served. Intermittently, the sound of the guitar played by Anjana's son Kunal is heard. As the two ladies discuss the sad plight of the cancer patients who are brought to the hospice Anjana volunteers for, their conversation is interrupted by the ringing of the door bell and the entry of Prabhakar, the nervous, awkward employee of Mr. Padabidri. He claims he has been called directly to the house for a meeting. As he waits, Prabhakar annoys the two ladies with his life story, his childhood in the Western Ghats and how, coming from a quiet area, he actually craves for the rhythms of traffic, construction noises, and large crowds in the city.

The play comprises the story of deceit of Prabhakar by Dolly who makes a show of benevolent high-class lady, having contacts with the eminent personalities like Azim and Yasmeen of IT industry. On her suggestion, he resigns his job, takes the loan of seventy thousand, sells his village land for the preliminary expenditure, pays two months' salary as a penalty to the company and arrives for an interview to get a job at Wipro in Singapore as the Regional Manager. But there is neither a job nor any prospects of getting the same in future. Naturally, it turns out to be a deception or a practical joke, bringing Prabhakar on a street.

The plot moves forward in a maze-like shape with parallel sub-plots, meeting and parting ways abruptly. The play deals with the life-stories of such characters as Anjana, Dolly, Kunal, Vimala, Muttu and Anusaya Padabidri.

The play ends with Anjana weeping over the loss of the magnificent rain-tree, Dolly again cheating someone by offering a foreign job, her husband Brigadier Iyer slapping her for it and her calmly bearing it as though she is used to it, Kunal informing Anjana of his Grandma's parting with all her money and jewellery on horse races, Anjana's narrating him the story of her friendship with a Bengali boy with whom she used to give the public programmes of Hindi film songs as well as those of Rabindra Sangeet, her unsuccessful attempt at suicide along with him (Kunal), her losing of voice and again regaining it when a demand to sing a song is made by a dying patient and Kunal describing Bengaluru as "Big Black Hole" (80).

It is an open-ended play as it lets most of its conflicts stay unresolved and the story deliberately leaves the audience without a denouement. The vague but open ending of the play contributes to convey the chaotic atmosphere of the much discussed and famous city of Bengaluru, which remains the centre of attraction of the literates as well as the illiterates.

Characterization and Setting

What Karnad is able to achieve in his characterization is an almost total objectivity. The play offers the basic and essential complexity of human nature. Anjana Padabidri, the central character, appears stern, strong, managing and juggling with a lot of things in life but she becomes very sensitive when the magnificent rain-tree across the road near her house is cut down. Dolly is her close friend pretending to hail from a high class society but is actually a battered wife of Brigadier Iyer. A sophisticated, charming, lady outwardly turns out to be bold, ruthless in the deceit of simple, innocent folks. Prabhakar is the protagonist of the play, simple and straightforward, easily swayed away by any Tom, Dick and Harry. He hails from a typically rural background and arrives in the city of Bengaluru with dreams and aspirations. Prabhakar's wife is a typical cranky wife, who has attraction for the life in the metro-city and despises going back to the village. Kunal, the son of Anjana, looks at everything with a broader and mature perspective as well as with a modern outlook.

Vimala has worked in the house of Anjana Padabidri for eight years but is now under suspicion for having stolen from the house (and seems to be guilty, too) with the help of a number of men who are all her "first cousins". She is blatantly bold about her lies and is cunning in tackling the situation. The drama in her story presents the difficult lives of the city's domestic help. Her life-story seems to communicate the message: Morality and ethics become secondary, when one is forced upon with the basic task of sourcing the next day's meals.[4]

With Muttu and her family, the playwright throws light on the outdated customs and traditions in our society particularly those in the rural part as well as the attraction of those people for city-life and their aspirations which ultimately turn into chaos. However, the outwardly simple Muttu turns out to be wily and vicious while acquiring the position of Vimala.

Anusaya Padabidri, the mother-in-law of Anjana is portrayed as the bored grandmother who becomes hooked to betting on horses at the Derby races (a favorite pastime of Bengaluru's wealthy). However, she sweeps the audience with her ability to shift from the exciting race course scenes to her candid conversations with her grandson Kunal.

The play is a collage of people and families that are connected and live in the city of Bengaluru. They have different reasons to be there and thrive on their dreams and aspirations which they hope that the city will fulfil.

It shows that the city gives a lot to each character but takes away the innocence and much more. Actually, it is how each character moulds himself/herself according to the demands of city life. The give-and-take relationship between the people and the city goes unending. Some feel sad at the changing city, some simply accept it, and some do not even cast an eye on it. For some, living in the city makes them lonely, for others, it is a matter of survival, and for a few, it is a city of dreams.

The stage set broadly covers Anjana Padabidri's house with elite furniture, a gallery of the Bengaluru Race Course, Coffee shop, Prabhakar's apartment, the police station, house of Shankar in Karimangala town, the reception room of the Wipro office, the garden outside Anjana's house, Vimala's hut, Muttu's house in Bengaluru and her brother's dwelling in a village. This is quite a diverse set design to manage, which really poses a challenge for the director.

In a nutshell, it can be stated: "Girish Karnad's play is vibrant with moments of lyricism, cruelty, and laughter, as it deals with a host of characters, jostling together, clashing, getting entangled, or preying upon each other, in the city of 'Bangalore'."[5]

Critical Interpretation and Appraisal of the Play

The play focuses more on the characters than on the theme. It represents characters of various classes, castes and locales. However, the chief protagonist of the play is the city of Bengaluru, strongly affected by globalization. Once upon a time, it was a calm, green city, now it is converted into an overcrowded city of aspiration and frustration showing the vast negative impact of modernization. Shanta Gokhale opines: "The chief protagonist of *Boiled Beans on Toast* is the city of Bangalore, a throbbing organism spawned by globalization. The play holds a mirror to the fractured lives of its floating population which occupies a broad social spectrum from the struggler to the street-smart survivor, from the small-town aspirant to the elite. This is the city of wild hopes and dashed dreams, of disappointment and despair, of environmental destruction and rapid development."[6]

In the portrayal of his characters, Karnad remains a detached observer an impartial spokesman who neither judges nor philosophizes either for the city or for its residents. He has maintained a disinterested, totally objective viewpoint devoid of nostalgia and has projected them with an ironic detachment. The play neither depicts the glory of the bygone age nor does it criticize the rapid development of the city at the cost of the destruction of nature resulting in global warming. "It looks at the reality of the present with unblinking eyes. The only time Karnad allows himself to judge is at the end, when Anjana's musician son, Kunal, describes Bangalore as a 'Big Black Hole'" (80).[7]

The principle of anti-thesis is maintained throughout the play. It explores the contrast that lies between village and city; human relations guided by family and community ties and those governed by pragmatic considerations; the idea of home, ancestral legacy, etc. Shanta Gokhale very justifiably states: "Structurally, *Boiled Beans on Toast* works as a prose symphony, the dominant theme being configured through long and short movements.... Like much modern music, here too there are more dissonant than consonant notes."[8]

Conclusion

While summing up, one can say: although the play is a ruthless dissection of human nature, there is something more in it than this sheer ruthlessness. In addition to it, a subtle underlying tone of sensitivity and tenderness towards humanity as a whole is noticed as intermittent. If one delves deep into the meaning of the play, the seeds of basic human values can be noticed as sown everywhere. In Anjana's weeping over the axing down of the magnificent rain-tree, in Kunal's playing of guitar, in Ausaya's informing Kunal about Anjana's gifted divine voice, in her words of praise for it as well as her regret over the loss of her voice, one comes upon a great storehouse of human values.

Outwardly, the play appears realistic not only in the portrayal of its characters but also in its setting. The locale comprises the common places in the city of Bengaluru. However, Shanta Gokhale seems opposed to calling the play realistic in the conventional sense of the term. She states: "Although one might with reason label the play realistic, chiefly because its characters are drawn with great attention to socio-psychological truth, the play departs enough from the conventionally realistic play.... The realistic play belongs to a time when narratives could be woven around a single focus, allowing a sedate development from exposition to complication and then on to resolution. *Boiled Beans on Toast* belongs to a world of multiple misalignments. If its purpose is to encompass the heterogeneity of the lives and dreams that make the organism tick, it has no choice but to discard linearity and the idea of a satisfying resolution."[9] However, the success of the play lies in keeping the resolution suspended and making the audience introspective.

Notes

1. Girish Karnad, *Boiled Beans on Toast*. New Delhi: OUP, 2014, jacket of the book.

2. Shanta Gokhale, "Foreword". *Boiled Beans on Toast*. Girish Karnad. New Delhi: OUP, 2014, viii.
3. Priya Adarkar, "Blurb". *Boiled Beans on Toast*. *op. cit.*, 2014.
4. mumbaitheatre.com
5. Girish Karnad, *op. cit.*, jacket of the book.
6. Shanta Gokhale, "Foreword". *op. cit.*, vii.
7. *Ibid.*, vii-viii.
8. *Ibid.*, viii.
9. *Ibid.*

14

Driven Snow: Decentering the Centre

Introduction

Girish Karnad's play *Driven Snow* is totally different from his other plays in that Karnad here directly deals with the contemporary reality instead of deriving his theme, as is his usual practice, from history and/or myth. Besides, it is the only play with a non-Indian locale. Originally, the play was written in 1977 in Kannada. It was translated into English in 2001 by the playwright himself. The title of the play in its English version is quite different from that of the original. It is *Anjumillage* which means 'scared jasmine'. Thus, the play bears the title *Fearing Jasmine* by Anand Lal in his *Anthology of Indian Theatre*.[1]

The setting of the play is a small flat in a university town in England. The play depicts the post-colonial society in the two nations—England and India. Maya Pandit opines, "...it deals with a situation that is essentially post-colonial; namely, the exploration of the condition of exile from the motherland from within...."[2]

The play explores the psyche of the non-resident Indians, especially of those who went to England with some aspirations in their minds and hearts. However, Karnad here very skilfully fuses various themes into a harmonious whole. For the fuller interpretation of the play, a deconstructionist analysis seems to be apt which deals with the idea that the establishment of a new fresh centre of unity is based on the rejection of the previous one. The play, on the one hand, delineates the situation of the people who leave their motherland permanently in the hope that the new land will enable them to disown their past along with their identity, and, on the other hand, represents the condition of those people who can neither forget their past (to be more accurate who do not want to forget it) nor can let others forget it. Through the character of Gautam, Karnad represents the Indian guy who is living in the foreign land with the sheer purpose of academic progress. The signifiers in the play carry the message that meaning is always fluid, slippery; it is always in a state of flux. The new interpretation rejects the previous one and establishes itself further assuming that it can be challenged by a new one. However, "the signs get erased, yet they leave behind them traces that take one beyond the connotational paradigms".[3]

The Play's Theme and the Story

The play projects the two sorts of relationship, i.e. sister-brother relationship on the one hand and that of their lovers on the other. It presents the life of a non-resident Indian in England and a white girl who desirous of marrying the Indian guy. Satish, the protagonist of the play, goes to England and settles down there, loves Ann and has decided to marry her. Yamini, Satish's sister also is living in England in a separate house to have her lessons in painting. The play depicts the ambivalence and complexity in human relationships. It starts with the comic incident of the information pertaining to the proposed marriage of Harry and ends with the death of Yamini.

The play dwells on the politics of language like the one Karnad has dealt with in his monologue *Broken Images*. English here is used in the role of 'father-tongue' as against the use of mother-tongue. It is a powerful weapon to enrich and empower one's personality. The use of English signifies the exile, signalling the loss of the mother-tongue imposed by the colonialists. English language is also one of the dominant motifs in the play and its perfect use points to the intellectual attainment of the user. The immigrant who has chosen to settle in the country of the colonizers has to master their language in order to get 'assimilated' into the new-found culture. Then only he/she can gain acceptance, which ultimately leads to getting married to a white girl/boy. However, the gaining of strength as an NRI ultimately results into the erasure of one nativist sign, viz. the mother-tongue, here.

The play, thus, starts with the consciousness of the dominance of the father-tongue over the mother-tongue. The English consciousness prevails upon the nativist one. But the stay in England does not lead to the intellectualization of an existential condition. It is not a play about the exiled Indians who want to return to their nation, but cannot, because of personal problems or socio-political conditions. On the contrary, it is a play about those Indians who are permanently settled in their newly adopted homeland and who are least inclined to return to their motherland. This decision raises several questions: Why don't they wish to go back? How do they perceive the land of their oppressors? What is their relationship with the country of their origin? What does the motherland signify for them? If staying in England is an escape from something, what is it that they are trying to run away from? The play, thus, projects a fusion of memories and desires. It appears like a maze in which the characters get themselves entangled. Karnad's artistry is perceptible in his adept handling of the theme of the Asian diaspora in England in a quite different way. "The condition of exile from the motherland makes the play an expression of post-colonial consciousness all right, but it is singularly different from the established expressions in this tradition in both India and other diaspora writing."[4]

Characterization

Anti-thesis dominates the play. It is noticed in treatment of the events as well as in the delineation of the characters. At the surface level, the plot of the play revolves round the brother and sister relationship: Satish Rao and Yamini Rao. However, at the deep level, it explores four love relationships, viz. that of Satish and Ann, Satish and Yamini, Yamini and David, and Yamini and Gautam.

The name "Yamini" signifies a dark night. She is a budding painter. The literal meaning of the word "Satish" is the God of Truth. He is a scientist and works in the laboratory of a university town in England. Yamini and Satish form a binary opposition: Satish stands for truth, that is, glittering white and Yamini signifies dark night.

Gautam is an Indian student of Economics and is bent upon making a good academic career. The name "Gautam" signals renunciation, that is, 'nirvana'. He is a person who is on a quest for knowledge and longs to be the life-partner of Yamini by seeking her hand in marriage.

Ann Burton is an English girl who loves Satish who, too, reciprocates her love and wants to marry her. Her whiteness is in contrast with Yamini's darkness. David is a right-wing racist and a chauvinistic Englishman. He hates Indians, since he thinks that they are responsible for creating the problem of unemployment in England.

Interestingly, the playwright here shows the turning of the tables. The once-upon-a-time rulers, the British, are now underdogs. It is the English land that is being now exploited by the outsiders, significantly, from the country that was once ruled by Britain. The "One" has turned into the "Other"— "...the 'Other' of the now obsolete Empire, evoking memories of loss and the abhorrence of impotence."[5] The shifting of the ruler-ruled role draws our attention to the truth: The exploited (the underdogs) are now in the position of exploiters (the upper dogs).

One character that never appears on the stage is Harren now Harry. He seems to be the most conspicuous character in the play by his sheer absence on the stage. With his life-story, Karnad has introduced a comic relief in the play, since the play begins with the account of his courting of a British girl, the opposition from her family and ends with the culmination of this love relationship into marriage. "But between the two events lies the entire vista of the dark world of the suppressed, brutal memories and the forbidden desires and passions, bringing along with them personal histories...."[6]

Critical Interpretation and Appraisal of the Play

The play begins in a light mood: two friends are gossiping about the marriage of Harry. He is the subject of fun and laughter for them. In order to become a part of the more developed society of the country of his adoption, he wants to get married to an English girl the daughter of a colonel. At the beginning, the characters of Satish and Harry appear similar. Actually, Harry seems to be the alter-ego of Satish. But, again, the centre is decentred. Somewhere in the heart of his heart, Satish feels guilty for leaving his motherland. He loves Ann, the English girl and, like Harry, wants to marry her. But unlike Harry, he wants her "*to see India first; realise what she is getting into*" (5). It throws light on the fact that he cannot snap his intimate bond with his native roots.

The play projects nativist vis-à-vis diasporic consciousness through its characters and situations. Satish comes to England with a decision never to return to his motherland. Gautam visits the country for academic progress. Yamini is living there with a blank mind. She dislikes Gautam and considers him a plague.

Yamini has a pessimistic picture of India in her mind, whereas, for Ann, the Indians are human, egalitarian, without any notions of hierarchical power relations. She bears a grudge against the English society which, in her view, is divided on the basis of class and colour consciousness. This impression is gathered through her opinions about the young men from the English public schools and that from the grammar schools. She thinks that the high class, rude and snobbish young men from the English public schools, look down even upon their fellow countrymen, the proletariats from the grammar school. For Ann, India stands free from such notions of class-consciousness and the snobbery that goes with it. However, her perception of India's image gets shattered through her association with Yamini. "If Ann is expected to know India through her interaction with Yamini, then the India that comes across is suddenly a smouldering nebula of unsuspected violence."[7]

Exile for Yamini is tantamount to an encounter with death. It goes through a cycle of—death-rebirth, regeneration, replantation, with a purpose of 'bursting', 'exploding' into flowers of life. She tries to scare Ann with her explanation:

> *If the jasmine plant refuses to bloom, do you know what they do? They uproot it.... They threaten it with death. Then they replant it and it bursts into flowers.* (8)

But who actually is in exile?—is a million dollar question left for the audience to ponder over.

The play represents the complex web of relationships, that is, Yamini-Satish, Yamini-David, Yamini-Gautam, Yamini-Ann and Satish-Ann. These relationships "create divergent conglomeration of the meanings of being in exile, all the while opening up several versions of India and being Indian, being in exile and being reborn on the face of it".[8]

Outwardly, the play seems to narrate the life-story of a brother and sister. The sojourn in London does not bring any substantial change in Satish's way of thinking, feeling and behaving. Actually, he appears to be a typical patriarchal Indian male who, with his dictatorial attitude, takes his sister for granted. Yamini, at the beginning, seems to be the replica of a typical Indian sister who loves her brother and is very caring about him.

However, the later part of the play represents her as a very strong and dominating character. There is a shifting of role here: from the role of a caring sister to that of a protective and possessive mother. Satish is fed up with her queries and gets annoyed at her crossing the limits as a caring sister. But he is too helpless to do anything against it. The playwright deliberately leaves the situation ambiguous and poses several intriguing questions such as: Why do they live in separate houses? What is it that is concealed in his past that renders him loveless and indifferent to his motherland and also to his parents? Why does he want Ann to know India through Yamini before getting married to him? Living in England and getting married to a white girl, is he trying to find an escape route to forget his past in India? Satish, with his diasporic consciousness, is the representative of all expatriates who decide to lead the life of exile forever. What does India signify for such young guys? Then, does Yamini symbolize mother India who never allows her son in exile to have a peace of mind and keep them constantly engaged in probing and analysing?

Through Yamini, Karnad seems to project the conservative, narrow-minded nativist psychology of Indian women who probably do not allow the outsiders to enter into the family. It may be for this reason that she tries to create hurdles in the marriage of Satish and Ann by narrating to Ann his affairs with various girls and passing vitriolic comments about his girlfriends. However, to malign her brother's image is not her intention. Actually, it indicates her desperate effort to keep her brother tied to their own community. "She becomes the manifestation of the caste-conscious Indian 'community' that tries to protect itself against the contamination of 'outsiders' coming into the family."[9]

But this centre of protective sister again gets decentred by her action of stepping towards the bedroom of Satish when he was with Ann, her pleading with Gautam to take her home, when she is well aware of the fact that Satish and Ann are probably sharing the bed. It signifies something more than the mere community or caste-consciousness and fear against the foreigners. Her poisoning of the ears of both Satish and Ann against each other by narrating to them the stories of the past life brings to surface the burning and unbearable reality that she is in the role of his beloved. It is for this reason that she cannot bear any girl's entry into the life of her brother.

Therefore, it seems that the main reason of Satish's exile from his motherland is Yamini. Maya Pandit's reflection in this regard goes, thus: "If Yamini symbolizes the land, and the land is 'disease', his (Satish's) desire to get distanced from her and the country becomes all the more justifiable.... He has to metaphorically 'die'...."[10]

Yamini and Satish both have the memories of their incestuous relationship with a slight difference: that Satish has been trying his best to forget and to cut off his past while Yamini has always been trying to keep it alive. It is for this reason that she cannot get married to Gautam nor does she want Satish to get married to Ann. Ann also notices her burning passion for Satish when a violent quarrel takes place between Satish and David.

Yamini, for Satish, is the sum of all womanly care: a sister, a mother and a beloved. Ultimately, the pure, serene sister-brother, mother-son relationship had been transformed into an illicit love relationship where illegitimate passions lead them to develop incestuous relationship. For Satish, it is a period of transition from childhood to adulthood. The close proximity, the unwarranted intimacy results into Yamini's pregnancy. The play indicates that anything can happen in man-woman relationship. The lust for passion renders a man blind. The new relationship makes Satish enter into the world of deceit, treachery and escape. Somehow, he manages for the abortion and leaves India for London.

> *He arranged for an abortion. Then he moved away... That's when I needed his warmth, ...* (67)

Therefore, living in England, Satish has been trying to escape his guilt-ridden past and also that of Yamini. It also unravels the mystery of their coming to England as well as that of their staying in different houses and also his insistence that she should return to India.

However, the audience are once again left in doubt to ponder over the probabilities: Is it a reality, a confession or a new strategy of deceit played by Yamini to scare Ann away from Satish? "Is it the innocent infatuation of a sister...? ...who is "*jasmine plant*" (8) that is uprooted and threatened with death? Is it Satish or is it Ann, who attempts suicide after listening to Yamini's disclosure or is it Yamini who lashes her wrists, saying "*I must show that white slut,*"—(71) trying to show her how to die? And which 'soil' are they going to get rooted in after being uprooted, so as to be reborn?"[11]

In the fragile world of the brother and sister, Karnad has also introduced the world of white fascist lorry drivers, violent and 'virile' through the character of David. He is one who seeks sadistic pleasure by torturing the coloured people. All Indians for him are either the "*wogs*" or the "*Packies*" (27). He wants his motherland "*Britain White!—White as 'driven snow'*" (31) without any black and non-whites dotting its clean surface.... "Yamini's affair with David signifies the process by which Yamini is made to die a thousand deaths—humiliation, self-torture, probably physical abuse along with invectives, and yet a strange kind of identification of David with the country she has left behind."[12] It also seems that her developing a relationship with the white man is a kind of revenge sought against Satish who has taken a decision to marry a white-skinned girl.

The play projects the plight of those, who choose to cross the borders of motherland and venture to settle down in a foreign land as well as of those who also choose to cross the borders, by breaking the taboos within India. A short and fleeting inter-caste love-story of a Brahmin woman with a Dalit boy brings to surface the problem of caste and community in India. David's bashing up of two Pakistanis, the floating body, in the well of an Indian woman for loving a Dalit man, and the horrible punishment of castration meted out to the man by the woman's husband for the crime of having loved a higher caste Brahmin woman bring to notice the burning reality that the problem of class, caste and community has persisted since the time immemorable in every country.

The play ends with several questions. Satish's explanation to Ann about Yamini's narrative clears the mist of deceit and treachery. His information that the house was sold when Satish was just five opens up another probability that Yamini's information about their childhood days is nothing but her own phantasmagoria/a figment of imagination upon which she has built up the edifice of her love-story. Similarly, her speaking with God also indicates her fragile psychological state and it seems that she may be suffering from schizophrenia. But the mind is caught in the web of query: What is the reality? If Yamini's narrative is just a figment of her illness, then why does Satish get petrified, when he casts a glance at Ann's sari, a birthday-gift to her by Yamini? The play is open-ended. The audience are left to arrive at their own interpretations. Towards the end of the play is the beginning of the audience's consciousness.

At the end of the play, Ann is left to make a choice. Satish wants her to know India through Yamini before getting married to him. The picture of India as painted by Yamini develops a view: "India would then mean unholy memories."[13]

Conclusion

Karnad, like that of in *Wedding Album*, here exhumes the reality of Indian culture. He once again denigrates the stereotyped Indian cultural norms and the conventional purity of familial relationship. The play is a ruthless dissection of Indian culture which is considered to be high and lofty, pure and serene. It is for this reason that Ann cannot allow the past memories of India alive either for her or for Satish. She proves herself to be a saviour by her decision of accepting him as her life-partner with all his positive and negative traits and also makes him accept her as she actually is: a white English lady. "*Let me begin being what I am*," (74) she declares and calls herself "*white*" (74). The play ends with the authorial voice, saying: "She is 'pure' like the white driven snow; but she might also be 'drifting' like the snow; who knows? Coldness of the driven snow also displaces the fragrance of the original jasmine."[14]

Karnad's scathing criticism of Jawaharlal Nehru's era is perceptible in this play also like the one we come across in *Tughlaq*. The play slightly hints at it. Yamini emphasizes the need of the young guys to return to India, saying "*Ours is a newly independent country and it is hungry for economists*" (9). On the contrary, Gautam thinks that the then Nehruvian socialist economy is "*a snarl of bureaucracy and corruption.... In any case, Nehru's India needs engineers and mechanics, but not 'pure scientists'...who want to be paid to speculate!*" (5)[15]

Towards the end of the play, it seems that the entire play centres on Ann. It depicts her story of being uprooted for getting married with a coloured Indian and again re-rooted in her own soil for her survival. The outwardly sensitive, delicate, submissive Ann turns out to be an iron-willed woman towards the end of the play, who successfully tries to make her lover to accept her as she is and remains victorious in it, since "he looks up at her" (74). She makes him believe: "She has to be herself, she is to be white. She has to be 'pure'."[16]

The play seems to throw light on the complexity of familial relationships. Yamini-Satish story deals with various themes such as—'mother' and 'motherland', 'woman' and 'incest'.

It brings out the sinister, frightening and dark side of man-woman relationship, while Ann-Satish story that culminates in their union highlights the fact that true love and purity of mind dissolve the boundaries of caste, class, community, and nation.

Notes

1. Anand Lal, Ed. *The Oxford Companion to Indian Theatre.* Delhi: OUP, 2004, 197.
2. Maya Pandit, "The Flickering Play of Desire and Memory: Exploring *Driven Snow*". *Girish Karnad's Plays: Performance and Critical Perspective.* Ed. Tutun Mukherjee. New Delhi: Pencraft International, 2006, 318.
3. *Ibid.*, 319.
4. *Ibid.*
5. *Ibid.*, 321.
6. *Ibid.*
7. *Ibid.*, 322.
8. *Ibid.*, 323.
9. *Ibid.*, 324.
10. *Ibid.*
11. *Ibid.*, 326-27.
12. *Ibid.*, 325.
13. *Ibid.*, 327.
14. *Ibid.*
15. *Ibid.*, 321.
16. *Ibid.*, 327.

EPILOGUE

15

Girish Karnad: A New Playwright

"The Theatre should not lie."

—Emile Zola

"Girish Karnad is a new playwright." "The motto of the new art...is, in one word, truth, and truth...is what we are striving for." The drama is, in its origin and nature, essentially didactic: It gives us a message, like Aesop's fable. The Karnad drama is "modern" in the sense that it is a journey from realism to ritualism. Variety and complexity, tradition and modernity, objectivity and contemporaneity are its greatest hall-marks. Like Chekhov, he, too, can claim: "I have not introduced a single villain nor an angel.... I accused nobody, justified nobody." Thus, the new drama, as conceived by Girish Karnad, is characterized by the Arnoldian twin virtues of literature, viz. "Truth and Disinterestedness," says L.S. Despande, my mentor.

Girish Karnad delves deep into his traditional Indian myths to spell out modern man's predicament, anguish, and dilemma. Karnad's plays are a critique of history, myth, and tradition; they are marked by contemporaneity and modernity. By using myths, he throws light on the reality of life with all its elemental passions and conflicts and also on man's eternal struggle to achieve perfection.

In Karnad's plays, we have glimpses here and there of such great Western playwrights as Camus, Sartre, Beckett, and Brecht. One can still feel a superb touch of Indianness in his plays. The folk forms such as *kathakali, dashavatara*, etc., and the modes of recitation and story-telling specific to the region, some trends in the Sanskrit theatre such as *nandi*, i.e. a play's beginning with a prayer to Lord Ganesha and *sutradhara,* i.e. a character that plays a role akin to that of the chorus in Greek drama have been used effectively. Thus, Karnad's theatre may be said to have bridged the gulf between the traditional and the modern Indian theatre. The plays, in general, display their author's social concern and commitment. Instead of providing an escapist way reflected in their amusing scenes and situations, they dwell upon the presentation of the problems pertaining to social inequality, anguish, and disillusionment in modern life, and the place of the individual in society.

It is observed that in Karnad's writing, there is a perfect synthesis of Eastern and Western dramaturgy, classical and folk conventions with which he creates a rich and vibrant drama rooted deep in tradition but with a resonant contemporary voice. Although his theatre is manifest in three independent forms or traditions that is, (a) the Sanskrit, (b) the Folk, and (c) the Modern, it has a distinctive unity behind its rich diversity. It is remarkable for its rich variety and complexity. So, his plays can be studied pre-eminently as modern with an awareness of the classical and folk elements interspersed in them.

Karnad is an individualist and, as such, presents the problem of an individual versus society. Thus, he stands for individual freedom. Having pinned his faith in the related values, he has been recognized as a pioneer of New Drama. His plays put forth several questions without providing any answers to them. The playwright seeks to present the modern man with his predicament, his challenges, his difficulties, and ramifications. The life seen around is projected as it is objectively and dispassionately and the dramatist makes no effort to moralize or philosophize it.

In Karnad's plays, one can clearly perceive existential and absurd strains. The characters in his plays are themselves responsible for shaping their existence and carving out their destinies. His first play *Yayati* strikes a note of angst and responsibility. To fulfil his ambition, King Yayati succeeds in transferring his old age as well as his sins to his younger son Pooru. However, in the process, he experiences shattering disillusionment and loss of faith which lead him towards alienation. It is this sense of responsibility that renders him restless and makes him feel dejected. Karnad states:

> I was excited by the story of *Yayati*. This exchange of ages between the father and the son which seemed to me terribly modern. At the same time, I was reading a lot of Sartre and the existentialists. This consistent harping of responsibility which the existentialist indulge in, suddenly seemed to link up with the story of *Yayati*.[1]

V.S. Khandekar, the renowned Marathi novelist, regards *Yayati* "as the representative of the modern man who, in spite of much varied happiness, is always discontented and is blindly running in the pursuit of new pleasures."[2] Towards the end of the play, Yayati becomes conscious of the fact that "to be is to live,...to live is to be responsible and to be responsible is to be moral."[3] It is due to this realization that he returns his newly acquired youth to Pooru and accepts the forest-life of *vanaprasthasharm*.

The plays such as *Tughlaq* and *Tale-Danda* are considerably branched off to history. But they are ahistorical in nature. History is used to interpret contemporary reality. In *Tughlaq*, Karnad explores the paradox of Muhammad bin Tughlaq, the idealistic Sultan of Delhi whose reign is considered to be one of the most spectacular failures in Indian history. The play actually symbolizes Jawaharlal Nehru's idealism. It is the story of an idealist dreamer who in his attempt to establish an ideal kingdom becomes conscious of the absurdity of human existence. Critics are of the opinion that the existential overtones connect *Tughlaq* with *Caligula* of Camus at the thematic level.[4] The play begins with the idealist phase of a monarch and ends with the bitter acceptance of his utter failure. In his attempt to create heaven on the earth, he brings about a situation which is worse than hell.

Both the plays *Tughlaq* and *The Dreams of Tipu Sultan* are concerned with the Islamic rulers. While the former deals with the medieval tyrannical rule of Muhammad bin Tughlaq, the latter throws light on the early days of colonialism and the various facets of Tipu's personality and his great concern for India. Both the plays bring out the distinction between the dreams and actions of the two protagonists who have the high goal of building a glorious kingdom that ended in a reign of terror and consequent violence. In *Tughlaq*, Karnad tries to maintain fidelity to the historical sources which present the Sultan as a combination of opposites—a dreamer and a man of action, benevolent and cruel, devoted to religion and secularism. Karnad deftly exploits history for raising social, religious and political issues of the age that seem to have a direct bearing on the present socio-political and religious scenario, to use Eliots oft-quoted phrases "the presence of the past" and "the pastness of the present".

In a nutshell, these plays are seen exploring the weaknesses of power politics. Outwardly, they appear historical; in reality, they are based on just a particular historical incident or a current situation. Nevertheless, they are least topical and have a universal appeal. The ideas treated therein are relevant to all times and climes. The situations depicted and the characters portrayed in these plays are beyond time and space.

It is observed that *Yayati*, Karnad's first play focuses on the problem of patriarchy in the ancient Indian context. It draws our attention to the problem of the unequal, reverential and somewhat tyrannical power relationship. The complex psychological and emotional world of Sharmishtha, Devayani and Chitralekha in *Yayati,* Padmini in *Hayavadana,* the Queen Amritamati in *Bali: The Sacrifice,* Rani in *Nagamandala,* Vishakha and Nittilai in *The Fire and the Rain* reveals the problem of women in patriarchy, marked by male-dominance. Though they belong to the ancient times, they may be seen as the representatives of the present generation of Indian women. Being subjugated and deprived of freedom, they challenge the patriarchal system and the implicit code of conduct.

Of all women characters in Karnad, Padmini is the most dynamic one. It is she who challenges the patriarchy and tries to realize her dream of "complete" man, but in vain. The play deals with the theme of emergence of a "New Woman" and a quest for completeness. Through the character of Padmini, Karnad represents a bold, iron-willed woman who goes against the tradition to fulfil her desire of having a husband who carries a superior head on a superior body. Padmini's predicament seems to be the predicament of a modern sophisticated woman of "women's lib". However, in the course of time, she realizes the absurdity of her efforts. The play also deals with the theme of the quest for identity in the world of tangled relationships. According to Prof. R.S. Sharma:

> That completeness is a humanly impossible ideal is suggested first in the story of *Hayavadana* and later in the transposition of heads. By showing the absurdity of the ideal of completeness, the play finally achieves its aesthetic goal. It implicitly asserts the value and significance of human imperfection which makes any upward movement possible.[5]

In *Nagamandala*, Karnad explores the position of woman in society. Rani, the central character is the victim of male-dominated society. Appanna, her husband, enjoys extra-marital relationship with a concubine quite openly and tries to punish Rani severely for sleeping with Naga who appears in the home in the form of Appanna. The village elders also ask Rani to prove her chastity by taking an ordeal. Appanna goes unquestioned, even unnoticed. Similarly, the play delineates the character of Rani, her transformation from an innocent, shy, and timid, girl into a clever, determined, emotionally well-controlled, rational woman. She seems to be an extension, a revised version of Padmini in the *Hayavadana*.

The age-old problem of the caste system also seems to be one of the major concerns of Karnad. Tughlaq fights against his Muslim enemies, whereas Tipu fights against the British forces. But *Tale-Danda* depicts a more horrible aspect of Indian history and society focusing on the ugly reality of the caste system in India. The society, depicted in the play is divided on the basis of caste, class, colour and gender. Inequality, violence, and exploitation characterize it. Basavanna, a saintly figure, had started his social movement in the twelfth century in Karnataka to build a casteless society. With his missionary zeal, he wanted to build up a democratic society based on the principles of freedom, justice, equality and fraternity. The orthodox Hindus were deadly opposed to the *sharana* movement. All the sincere efforts of Basavanna to create a casteless society come to nothing, when he performs an inter-caste marriage of a Brahmin girl with a cobbler boy. But Basavanna's dream of creating a casteless society ends in violence at last.

Although the play is based on one of the incidents of the 12th century, it reflects contemporary burning reality that despite all the efforts of the social activists in India, our society has been still "broken into fragments by narrow domestic walls". Karnad states:

> The whole thing (the story) does not seem very different from 1991. It is a kind of exploration for what might have happened. Why is that some of our problems seemed perennial? That's why I wrote *Tale-Danda*.[6]

The problem of caste system is also raised in *Yayati* and *The Fire and the Rain.* The petty quarrel between Devayani and Sharmishtha becomes the root-cause of their enmity and generates bitterness between them. This trivial incident of quarrel takes a form of perpetual war of race, caste, and class. In *The Fire and the Rain*, the low caste people are prohibited to enter the place of the Fire Sacrifice. The play explores the deep gulf between the lower and the upper caste people.

Coming to the last plays in the present volume, the monologue *Flowers* explores the problem of sin and merit in the priest's life. It is a legendary tale transformed into a wonderful drama, with a tragic end. Sex and devotion are juxtaposed with each other in the love story.

The play *Broken Images* is also a monologue that probes the darker side of the play's female protagonist Manjula Nayak. Her identity is established through the voice of conscience reflected in the speeches of her own image.

In the play *Wedding Album*, Karnad creates a new myth and presents, through the delineation of the characters and the events, a few glimpses of the contemporary Indian reality. It simultaneously represents the East-West encounter with its native and the exotic elements and the never-ending conflict between tradition and modernity. The architechtonics of drama provides a specimen of culture study in the artistic form—evoking both the types of imagination, auditory and visual. It is a strong indictment on the modes of thinking, feeling and behaving of the contemporary society.

The last but one play *Boiled Beans on Toast* dwells on the nativist consciousness giving us a brilliant saga of the south Indian city of Bengaluru. It is a realistic play presenting a world of "multiple misalignments". The play holds a mirror to the people with their "fractured lives"—moving to and fro in the city of Bengaluru.

The last of the plays *Driven Snow*, is the best. It is a post-colonial, deconstructionist play that projects a contrast between the nativist and the diasporic consciousness.

The problem of inequality, the position of woman in the society, absurdity of human existence appear to be the major themes of Karnad's plays. However, the playwright is not given to any particular trend, nor does he take any avowedly philosophical or ideological stance such as absurdity, or existentialism, or naturalism or individualism or socialism. In most of his plays, women play roles as prominent as men. He is not a downright feminist, however. There is, nevertheless, a fine blend of all these ideological inclinations and/or tendencies in his plays. He is, therefore, a committed but "committed" in the existential sense of that word—"committed" to the higher values of life that go to the making of humanity. He is, in one word, "a great humanist".

In conclusion, one can say: like Shakespeare, Girish Karnad is, at once, both—a playwright and a player, par excellence, and his plays pleasant and unpleasant provide a brilliant commentary on the life that is lived and being lived in "high seriousness", compelling us to say, quite cheerfully, and wonderously: "O brave new world, that has such people in it!"

Notes

1. Rajinder Paul, "Girish Karnad Interviewed". *Enact*, 54.
2. Y.P. Kulkarni, (Translator). "*Yayati* by Karnad" Translated and abridged from Marathi. New Delhi: Orient Paperbacks (1978).

3. Sharad Asolkar, "Astitwawad ani Sartre". *Yugwani*. Ed. Sharad Kolarkar. May 1980, 19.
4. C.H. Ravindranath, *The Myth in the Plays of Girish Karnad: A Thematic Study*. An M.Phil. Dissertation. Submitted to Kakatiya University, Warangal 1992, 67.
5. R.S. Sharma, "Karnad's *Hayavadana*". *Literary Criterion*. 13, 1978, 69.
6. Monthushi Chakravarthy, "To Karnad". *Tenor*. Sept. 1991. Quoted in C.H. Ravindranath, *op. cit.* 12.

Note: The page numbers indicated in the brackets in the entire work refer to the following texts:

(i) Girish Karnad, *Boiled Beans on Toast*. New Delhi: OUP, 2014.

(ii) Girish Karnad, *Collected Plays*. Volume One and Two. New Delhi: OUP, 2005.

(iii) Girish Karnad, *The Fire and the Rain*. New Delhi: OUP, 1998.

(iv) Girish Karnad, *Wedding Album*. New Delhi: OUP, 2009.

(v) Girish Karnad, *Yayati*. New Delhi: OUP, 2008.

The play *Driven Snow* is still unpublished. Courtesy to playwright for giving the manuscript of this play.

Appendix

Girish Raghunath Karnad

Early Life and Education

Place of Birth	:	Matheran (Maharashtra)
Education	:	B.A. (Mathematics and Statistics), Karnatak Arts College, Karnatak University, Dharwad, 1958.
		M.A. (Philosophy, Political Science, Economics) Lincolon and Magdalen College, Oxford University, Oxford, 1960-63.
Specialization	:	B.A. Ranked first in the university, 1958.
		Dakshina Fellow in the Department of Statistics for M.A., Bombay University, Bombay. (Due to the stay at Oxford, the M.A. Degree remained incomplete), 1958-60.
		Rhodes Scholarship, Oxford, 1960-63.
		Frere Exhibition, Magdalen College, 1962-63.
		Chairperson, Magdalen College, Junior Common Room, 1962-63.
		Chairperson, Oxford Union Society, 1963.
Career	:	Assistant Manager and then Manager, Oxford University Press, Madras, 1963-70.
		Director, Film and Television Institute, Pune, 1974-75.
		Director, Nehru Centre, London
		Secretary, Indian High Commission 2000-03

Awards and Honours

1958	Ranked first in the university in B.A.
1958-59	Dakshina Fellow in the Department of Statistics for MA., Bombay University.
1960-63	Rhodes Scholarship, Oxford.
1962	Mysore State Award for *Yayati.*
1963	President, Oxford Union Society.
1970	Government of Mysore Rajyostsava Award.
1970	President's Gold Medal for the Best Indian Film for *Samskara.*
1970-72	Homi Bhabha Fellowship for creative work in folk theatre.
1972	Sangeet Natak Academy Award for playwriting.
1972	Kamaladevi Chattopadhyaya Award of the Bharatiya Natya Sangh for the Best Indian Play of the Year for *Hayavadana.*
1972	National Award for Excellence in Direction for *Vamsha Vriksha* (shared with B.V. Karanath).
1972	Mysore State Awards for the Best Kannada Film and Best Direction for *Vamsha Vriksha.*
1972	President's Rajtpadak for the film *Kaadu.*
1974	President's Silver Medal for the Second Best Indian Film for *Kaadu.*
1974	Padma Shri Award from the President of India.
1974-75	Director, Film and Television Institution, Pune.
1976-78	President, Karnataka Nataka Academy.
1978	National Award for the Best Kannada film for *Ondanondu Kaaladalli.*
1978	National Award for the Best Script for *Bhumika* (shared with Shyam Benegal and Satyadev Dubey).
1978	Filmfare Award for the Best Script for *Godhuli* (shared with B.V. Karnath).

1978 West Bengal Film Journalists Association Award for the Best Actor of the Year for *Swami.*

1978 West Bengal Sangha Award for Best Acting in the film *Manthan.*

1984 Karnataka Natak Academy Award.

1984-93 Indian Co-chairman, Joint Media Committee (for Films, Broadcasting and Press) of the Indo-US Sub-Commission on Education and Culture.

1987-88 Visiting Professor and Fulbright Scholar-in-Residence, University of Chicago.

1988-93 Chairman, Sangeet Natak Akademi, New Delhi.

1989 Nandikar, Calcutta, award for playwriting.

1990 Golden Lotus for the Best Non-Feature Film on Social Issues for *The Lamp in the Niche*

1990 "Writer of the Year" Award from *Granthaloka Journal* of the Book Trade for *Tale-Danda.*

1991 Karnatak State Award for the Best Supporting Actor in *Santa Shishunala Shareef.*

1992 B.H. Sridhar Award for *Tale-Danda.*

1991 Karnatak Sahitya Academy Award for the Most Creative Work of 1989 for *Nagamandala.*

1992 Karnatak Natak Academy Award for the Best Play of 1990-91 for *Tale-Danda.*

1992 Padma Bhushan Award from the President of India.

1992 Booksellers and Publishers Association of South India Award.

1993 Karnatak Sahitya Academy Award for *Tale-Danda.*

1993 National Award for the Best Film on Environment Conservation for *Cheluvi.*

1994 Doctor of Letters from Karnatak University, Dharwad.

1994 Special Honour Award from the Karnataka Sahitya Academy.

1994 Sahitya Academy Award for *Tale-Danda.*

1994	Elected Fellow, Sangeet Natak Akademi, New Delhi.
1997	Gubbi Veeranna Award by the Government of Karnataka.
1999	Kalidas Samman by the Government of Madhya Pradesh.
1999	Bharatiya Jnanpith Award.
2000-03	Director, the Nehru Centre, London and Minister, Culture, High Commission of India, London.
2010	Honorary D. Litt. by Vidyasagar University, Midnapur.
2011	Honorary D. Litt. by Ravansha University, Bhuvaneshwar.
2011	Honorary Doctorate of Humane, University of Southern California, Los Angeles, USA.

Plays

Kannada

Yayati, Manohara, Granthmala, Dharwad, 1960.

Tughlaq, Manohara, Granthmala, Dharwad, 1964.

Maa Nishaadha (One Act Play) (1964). Published in *Ekaanka Sangraha*, Ed. Sinduvalli Aanantha Murthy, New Delhi: Sahitya Akademi, 1986.

Hayavadana, Manohara, Granthmala, Dharwad, 1971.

Anjumallige, Manohara, Granthmala, Dharwad, 1977.

Hittina Hunja, Manohara, Granthmala, Dharwad, 1980.

Nagamandala, Manohara, Granthmala, Dharwad, 1989.

Tale-Danda, Manohara, Granthmala, Dharwad, 1991.

Agni Mattu Male, Manohara, Granthmala, Dharwad, 1994.

Tippuvina Kannasugalu, Manohara Granthmala, Dharwad, 2000.

Bimba Mattu itar Natakgalyu, Manohara Granthmala, Dharwad, 2004.

Maduveya Album, Manohara, Granthmala, Dharwad, 2006.

Odakalu Bimba, Manohara Granthamala, Dharwad, 2006.

Sagram Natak, Manohara, Granthmala Dharwad 2007.

Flowers, Manohara, Granthmala Dharwad, 2012.

Benda Kaalu on Toast, Manohara, Granthmala Dharwad, 2012.

English

Tughlaq, Oxford University Press, New Delhi, 1972.

Hayavadana, Oxford University Press, New Delhi, 1975.

Nagamandala, Oxford University Press, New Delhi, 1990.

Tale-Danda, Ravi Dayal Publishers,, New Delhi, 1993.

Three Plays: Nagamandala, Hayavadana, Tughlaq, Oxford University Press, New Delhi, 1994.

The Fire and the Rain, Oxford University Press, New Delhi, 1998.

The Dreams of Tipu Sultan, Oxford University Press, New Delhi, 2004.

Two Plays: The Dreams of Tipu Sultan, Bali: The Sacrifice, Oxford University Press, New Delhi, 2004.

Collected Plays, Vol. 1 (*Tughlaq, Hayavadana, Bali: The Sacrifice, Nagamandala*) Oxford University Press, New Delhi, 2005.

Collected Plays, Vol. 2 (*Tale-Danda, The Fire and the Rain, The Dreams of Tipu Sultan, Two Monologues: Flowers, A Heap of Broken Images*), Oxford University Press, New Delhi, 2005.

Yayati, Oxford University Press, New Delhi, 2008.

Wedding Album, Oxford University Press, New Delhi, 2009.

Boiled Beans on Toast, Oxford University Press, New Delhi, 2014.

Driven Snow, yet unpublished in English.

Feature Films

Samskara (Kannada): Script, Dialogues, Lead Role, 1969.

Vamsha Vriksha (Kannada): Script, Acting and Direction (with B.V. Karanth), 1971.

Kaadu (Kannada): Script, Direction, 1973.

Godhuli (Hindi): Script, Direction (with B.V. Karanth), 1977.

Ondanondu Kaaladalli (Kannada): Story, Script, Direction, 1978.

Utsav (Hindi): Script, Direction, 1984.

Woh Ghar (Television play in Hindi) Direction, 1986.

Cheluvi (Hindi): Script, Direction, 1992.

Kanooru Heggadithi (Kannada): Script, Direction and Lead Role, 1999.

Other Films

Nishant, 1975

Manthan, 1976

Swami, 1977

Umbartha, 1982

Ananda Bhairavi, 1983

Nagamandala, 1996

Pukar, 2000

Agni Varsha, 2002

Iqbal, 2005

Dor, 2006

*8*10 Tasveer*, 2009

Aashayein, 2010

Kempe Gowda, 2011

Ek Tha Tiger, 2012

Documentaries

D.R. Bendre (Kannada) on the Kannada poet, 1973.

Kanaka Purandara (English): on two Medieval Bhakti Poets of Kannada, 1988.

The Lamp in the Niche (English Part I-Sufisim in India, Part-II Sufism in Bhakti, 1989.

Bhagvad Gita: B.B.C. Channel Four, 2002.

Teleserials

Antaral, 1997

Swarajnama, 1998

Kanoor ki Thakurani, 1999

Malgudi Days (in the role of Swami's father), 1986-87.

Prose Writing

Aagomme Eegomme (Article Collection) Manohara Granthamala, Dharwad, 2008.

Aadaadta Aayushya (Autobiography in Kannada) Manohara Granthamala, Dharwad, 2011.

Khelata Khelata Aayushya (Autography in Marathi) Rajhans Prakashan, Pune, 2013.

Bibliography

Primary Sources

Karnad, Girish. *Boiled Beans on Toast*. New Delhi: OUP, 2014.

———. *Collected Plays*. Volume One and Two. New Delhi: OUP, 2005.

———. *Driven Snow*. Unpublished Manuscript (Courtesy to playwright).

———. *The Fire and the Rain*. New Delhi: OUP, 1998.

———. *Wedding Album*. New Delhi: OUP, 2009.

———. *Yayati*. New Delhi: OUP, 2008.

Secondary Sources

Abrams, M.H. *A Glossary of Literary Terms*. New Delhi: Macmillan, 2007.

Babu Sarat, Manchi. *Indian Drama Today: A Study in the Theme of Cultural Deformity*. New Delhi: Prestige, 1997.

Bamber, Gascoigne. *Twentieth Century Drama* (London: Hutchinson, 1962).

Bhatta, S. Krishna. *Indian English Drama: A Critical Study*. New Delhi: Sterling, 1987.

Dass, Veena Noble. *Modern Indian Drama in English Translation*. New Delhi: 1988.

Deshpande, L.S. *Samakaleen Bharatiya Rangabhumi* (Contemporary Indian Theatre M.S. in Marathi). Dissertation submitted to K.K. Birla Foundation, New Delhi: 2008.

Dhanavel, P. *The Indian Imagination of Girish Karnad*. New Delhi: Prestige, 2000.

Dharwadker, Aparna. *Introduction to Collected Plays*. Vol. I, New Delhi: OUP, 2005.

Dodiya, J.K. and K.V. Surendran (eds.). *Indian English Drama: Critical Perspectives*. New Delhi: Sarup and Sons, 2000.

Esslin, Martin. *Theatre of the Absurd*. London: Penguin, 1968.

Gagri, Balwant. *Theatre in India*. New York: Theatre Arts, 1962.

Gaskell, Ronald. *Drama and Reality*. London: Routledge and Kegan Paul, 1972.

Gowda, Anniah. *Indian Drama*. Mysore: Univ. of Mysore, 1974.

Kanwar, Asha S. *The Theatre of India*. Trans. Mukherji Narayan, 2 Vols., Calcutta: Writers Workshop, 1978.

Levi, Sylvain. *The Theatre of India*. Trans. Mukherji Narayan. Writers' Workshop, 1978.

Mee, Erin B. *Drama Contemporary*. New Delhi: OUP, 2002.

Murthy, K. Narasimha. *Modern Kannada Literature*. Bengluru: Pustakalya Publication, 1992.

Naik, M.K. and S. Mokashi Punekar (eds). *Perspectives on Indian Drama in English*. Madras: OUP, 1977

Nand, Kumar. *Indian English Drama: A Study in Myths*. New Delhi: Sarup and Sons, 2003.

Pandey, Sudhakar and Barua, Freya (eds.). *New Directions in Indian Drama*. New Delhi: Prestige, 1994.

———. *The Studies in Contemporary Indian Drama*. New Delhi: Prestige, 1990.

———. *G.B. Shaw: A Critical Response*. New Delhi: Prestige, 1992.

Prasad, A.N. et al. (eds.). *Studies in Indian Drama in English*. Bareilly: Prakash Book Depot, 2003.

Rangacharya, Adya. *Introduction to Bharata's Natyasastra*. Bombay: Popular Prakashan, 1966.

———. *The Indian Theatre*. New Delhi: Sahitya Akademi, 1971.

Tandon, Neeru (ed.). *Perspectives and Challenges in Indian English Drama*. New Delhi: Atlantic, 2006.

Tiwari, Shubha (ed.). *Contemporary Indian Dramatists*. New Delhi: Atlantic, 2007.

Vatsyaya, Kapila. *Traditional Indian Theatre: Multiple Streams*. New Delhi: National Book Trust, 1980.

Williams, Raymond. *Drama from Ibsen to Eliot*. London: Chatto, 1952.

Dissertations, Articles, Interviews, and Introductions

Anniah Gowda, H.H. "Indian Drama in English: Some Highlights". *Indian Writing in the New Millennium*. Ed. R.K. Dhawan. New Delhi: IAES, 1999.

Bhatta, Krishna S. "Indo-Anglian Drama: A Critical Study". *Triveni*. 52.3. 1983, 67-73.

Bhatta, Krishna S. "Indian English Drama: Models and Techniques". *Triveni*. 56.2, 1987, 31-35.

Chari, Jaganmohan and Renuka, E. "The Plays of Vijay Tendulkar". *New Quest*. Jan.-Feb., 1988, 27-28.

Dhawan, R.K. "Girish Karnad: The Man and the Writer". *The Plays of Girish Karnad: Critical Perspectives*. Ed. Jaydipsingh Dodiya. New Delhi: Prestige, 1999.

Dhawan, R.K. "New Directions in Indian Drama: A Report on the Seminar". *New Directions in Indian Drama*. Eds. Sudhakar Pandey and Freya Barua. New Delhi: Prestige, 1994.

———. "Introduction". *Three Modern Indian Plays*. New Delhi: OUP, 1989.

Hemadri, Usha. "The Relevance of Experimental Theatre". *Indian Post*. 2 Jul. 1989, 6.

Karnad, Girish. "Author's Introduction". *Three Plays*. Delhi: OUP, 1994.

Marulasiddappa, K. "Drama's Turning Point". Trans. Chaitanya. *Spectrum*. 11 Jun. 1994.

Moses, Sudha. *Anger and Commitment in the Post-War British Drama*. A Ph.D. Dissertation. Marathwada University, Aurangabad, 1970.

Pandit, Maya. "A Dark Continent: Modernity and Gender: Perception in Modern Indian Theatre". *Theatre India*. No. 17, May 2003.

Paul, Rajinder. "Modern Indian Theatre". *Seminar*. 359, 1989, 39-42.

Rai, R.N. "Perspectives and Challenges in Indian English Drama". *Perspectives and Challenges in Indian English Drama*. Ed. Neeru Tandon. New Delhi: Atlantic, 2006.

Shukla, Supriya. "Indian English Drama: An Introduction". *Perspective and Challenges in Indian English Drama*. Ed. Neeru Tandon. New Delhi: Atlantic, 2006.

Sundaraman, M.N. "Tradition and Modernity in Indian English Drama". *The Journal of Indian Writing in English*. 21.1, 1993, 1-13.

Tripathi, Vanashree. "*Hayavadana*: Towards Forging an Indian Theatre". *Three Plays of Girish Karnad: A Study in Poetics and Culture*. New Delhi: Prestige, 2004.

Yadava, Raju B. "Race and Gender in *Yayati*". *Girish Karnad's Plays: Performance and Critical Perspectives*. Ed. Tutun Mukherjee. New Delhi: Pencraft International, 2006.

Yadav, Saryug. "Indian English Drama: Tradition and Achievement". *Indian English Drama: Critical Perspectives*. Eds. J.K. Dodiya and K.V. Surendran. New Delhi: Sarup and Sons, 2000.

Index